RELIGIONS
OF THE WORLD

RELIGIONS OF THE WORLD

JAMES HASKINS

Revised Edition

Hippocrene Books
New York

Revised edition, 1991

Copyright © 1991, 1973 by James S. Haskins

All rights reserved.

Published in the Hippocrene Great Religions of the World
Series in 1991 by Hippocrene Books, Inc.

For information, contact:
HIPPOCRENE BOOKS, INC.
171 Madison Avenue
New York, NY 10016

ISBN 0-87052-930-7

Library of Congress Cataloging-in-Publication Data available.

Printed in the United States of America

To Elinor

Acknowledgements

I am grateful to Lolita Ali, Ann Kalkhoff, and Kathy Benson for their help with this book.

Contents

Religion is like the fashion. One man wears his doublet slashed, another laced, another plain; but every man has a doublet. So every man his religion. We differ about trimming.

John Selden, *Table-Talk: Religion* (a. 1654)

Introduction

WHO AM I? WHY WAS I BORN? DOES MY LIFE HAVE A purpose? Does the world have a purpose? When I die will I no longer exist? What is the meaning of it all? Man has asked these questions almost from the beginning of his history, and for just about as long, he has looked to religion for answers to these questions.

It is hard to define *religion*. Ten different people will give ten different meanings. For one person, religion is a complete way of life, determining what he eats, who his friends are, whom he marries, even his daily schedule. For another, religion means going to church or synagogue or temple and observing religious holidays. For another, religion is simply a way of living in the world; for another it is a belief in God. For still another, it is not a belief in God but a feeling of oneness with the universe. And for some, religion is just something practiced by other people, something that other people need to provide meaning for their lives.

Even those who would not call themselves religious agree that religion has played an important role in man's history. It has given mankind some of its greatest heroes and some of its greatest tragedies. The history of religion, like the history of man, is one of love and pride and joy and sorrow and pain and greed. As long as man survives, so will religion.

Five major religions are practiced in the world today and each is centuries old. Hinduism developed first, then Buddhism, Judaism, Christianity, and finally Islam. But they are not more or less important than other religions because they are older or newer. Their importance is that for centuries they have satisfied basic human needs and answered man's basic questions. The chief differences among them have to do with whose needs they satisfy and whose questions they answer. Within the human race there are many differences, and the most important difference, where religion is concerned, is the difference between Eastern and Western man.

Here the terms *Eastern* and *Western* do not really correspond to the Eastern and Western hemispheres, for the Western hemisphere wasn't "discovered" until well after all these religions had been born. Where religion is concerned, the terms *Eastern* and *Western* depend upon a man's view of life and his questions about it.

Hinduism and Buddhism are Eastern religions. Both arose in India, although Buddhism moved out of India and today is practiced chiefly in Southeast Asia. Hindus and Buddhists believe that there is no real meaning to human life and that the individual is not important. Their greatest fear is that life may continue in an endless cycle of births and rebirths on earth. Their greatest hope is that they will find a way to escape this eternal earthly life and unite with a universal spirit that is above meaninglessness and meaning. Both Hinduism and Buddhism provide ways of escape for believers.

By contrast, the Western religions—Judaism, Christianity, and Islam—are found among people who believe there must be meaning to human life. Their fear is that human life and individual men's lives are meaningless. Their hope is that they will find meaning. Judaism, Christianity, and Islam stress belief in one God with whom it is possible to communicate, who cares about those who believe in Him, whose worship can give meaning to the believer's life, and who can reward the believer with continued life after he dies on earth.

All of these religions have moved outside their countries of birth through migration of peoples and colonization, and all have changed their ideas and practices over the centuries as the needs of their devotees have changed. Today, all of these religions are still in a state of change. Increased communication among the peoples and countries of the world, scientific discoveries and theories that have called into question some religious beliefs, philosophies that argue that religion is not necessary—all these things threaten the five established religions. And yet, as we have seen in the second half of the twentieth century, the same things that threaten religions may also serve to revitalize them. An understanding of the five major religions helps to explain why.

I

Hinduism

HINDUISM IS THE OLDEST OF THE WORLD'S LIVING RE-
ligions. The term *Hinduism* comes from the Persian
word *Hindu*, meaning "Indian," and thus Hinduism is
the "ism," or system of belief and way of life, of the
Indian people. Actually, *Hinduism* is a Western term
for the religious beliefs and practices of the majority of
people in India. Hindus themselves call their religion
Sanatana Dharma—the ancient and eternal religion.

Hinduism has no founder and does not depend for
its existence on any single historic event. It has evolved
through the experiences of several people and has un-
dergone several transformations in its long history. Hinduism does recognize a Creator, called Brahma, but
Brahma is only a manifestation of Brahman, or Ultimate Reality. Unlike some other major religions, Hinduism has never claimed to be the only way to reach

Ultimate Reality. Hindus believe in all religions and in all routes to God.

Hinduism therefore recognizes many ways to worship. Hindus accept the concept of "to each according to his own need and capacity." Thus, ways of worship include devotion to particular gods such as *Vishnu*, the Protector, and *Aditya*, the Sun God, as well as meditation, the reading of sacred texts, and the singing of *bhajans* or devotional songs. In this way, Hinduism is accessible to all, from the illiterate to the scholar.

The main desire of a Hindu is not to become a perfect human being on earth or a happy dweller in heaven, but to become united with Brahman and to achieve Divine Perfection. In Brahman there are no differences or separations, no time and space, no good and evil, no joy and sorrow, no desires of any kind. In fact, in Brahman there is no sense of individuality, but only pure being, consciousness, and bliss.

A person cannot achieve freedom from the sense of individuality and separateness from the universe merely by living a life of goodness, charity, and humility. One can achieve this freedom only by completely changing one's way of thinking and of seeing the world.

One must aim to acquire certain virtues, the five most important of which are: purity, self-control, detachment, truth, and nonviolence. At the same time, one must suppress the six deadly sins or passions: desire or lust, anger, greed, infatuation, pride, and envy. Achieving these virtues and suppressing these passions is not possible in a single lifetime, and thus Hindus believe in reincarnation, or the transmigration of souls, the passing of individual souls from one life to another: the rebirth after death of a living being, as an animal or as a man or a woman, in a status either higher or lower than that of the previous existence. This cycle of births and deaths is called *samsara*, and one's status in the cycle is determined by *karma*.

Karma may be described as the sum of a person's thoughts and actions in all previous lives. In each life, one changes one's karma for either better or worse. According to the concept of karma, when—for instance—a Hindu merchant dies, his soul enters another life in a new person. If the merchant has lived a life of good moral deeds and self-discipline, he is reborn in a higher station of life. If he has lived a sinful life, he is reborn as a servant or some other person of lower status. The way he lived in the previous life determines the station into which he is born in the next.

The concept of sin in Hinduism differs from that in Christianity, for example. In Hinduism, one is not punished *for* one's sins but *by* one's sins. The merchant in our example is responsible for what he does. If he lives a sinful life, he condemns himself to a next life that is lower down in the scale of samsara.

The Hindu belief in the stages of existence is reflected in the social structure of India and in the life of the individual. In fact, Hinduism is a very complex, orderly system which covers all aspects of Indian life.

The History of Hinduism

The history of Hinduism extends over centuries, and its length and the lack of early documents about it make it difficult to trace exactly. India's religious history can only be very roughly divided into ancient, medieval, and modern periods.

There have been civilizations in India for at least 5,000 years. Archeological excavations in the Indus Valley reveal that the dark-skinned people of the Indus had well-developed industries, urban planning, and established religious beliefs that centered around worship of forces of nature like fire, wind, and rain. Two of the great Hindu gods, *Siva* and *Vishnu*, were being worshipped at least as early as 2500 B.C.

Around 2500 B.C., the Indus Valley was invaded from the East by Aryans, a light-skinned, warlike, illiterate people whose religion was similar to those of the Greeks, Romans, and Scandinavians of the time. It was based on three classes of gods—of the heavens, the atmosphere, and the earth. In like manner, the Aryan population was divided into three classes, each having special gods. In the highest class were the priests, whose special god was the fire god *Agni*. Next came the warriors (including kings or tribal chiefs) whose special god was the warrior god, *Indra*. Finally, the common people (peasants and craftsmen) worshiped the 'all-gods,' the divine people. All these gods were worshiped through animal and sometimes human sacrifice.

After conquering the Indus peoples militarily, the Aryans set about converting them to their religion, although the intermingling of the Indus and the Aryans resulted in a religion that bore the marks of belief systems from both. The primary means of establishing this religion was through the Vedas, four collections of prayers, sacred rites, and discussions of life and death. The Vedas arose around 2000 B.C., and were at first handed down orally. They were not created by any single person or group, but for a long time they were uttered only by the Brahmans, or priests.

The Vedas expanded the three-class system of the Aryans to include the native population, and the Hindu caste system was born. In Hindu, they are called *varnas*. Varna means color, and the castes at first followed racial lines. All the castes were believed to be descended from Braham, the Creator, and to have sprung from parts of his body. From his head came the Brahmans, or priests; from his arms, the warriors; from his thighs the merchants and craftsmen; and from his feet the menial workers. Slaves were not included in this caste system and were designated by the terms outcaste and untouchable and Harijan.

Naturally, it took centuries for this system to be imposed all over the Indus valley, and migration and intermarriage have always prevented absolute caste boundaries. But the freely developed caste system was remarkably strict and governed most aspects of life. Each caste was a self-contained community; members of one caste were not permitted to intermarry or even to eat, drink, or smoke with members of another. Each caste had its own rituals and customs and its members were not permitted to practice those of other castes. Each had certain occupations, those regarded as dirty or "polluting"—such as hair-cutting, delivering babies, and lavatory cleaning—being reserved for low castes. The outcastes or untouchables suffered most from this system. They were forbidden to enter public buildings used by their betters, had to draw water from different wells and often to travel on different paths, and had to live in hamlets remote from the villages they served.

The life of each man in the three higher classes was divided by the Vedas into four stages, providing that he went through the ceremony of initiation. After the initiation, when he was a young boy, he became a student. Next he was a householder producing sons and fulfilling his family duties. In later middle age, when he had seen his grandchildren, he retired—ideally to a hut in the forest—and devoted his life to meditation. Finally, as an old man he became a homeless, religious beggar, giving up all earthly comforts. This life plan has always been more of an ideal than an actual practice, as it could never be enforced by law like the caste system.

The religion set forth by the Vedas was fine for the three higher castes. But for the servant caste, the conquered peoples, it contained no hope, no way to better themselves. Seemingly in answer to their needs, the Upanishads were created about the fifth century B.C. It is in the Upanishads that the influence of the religion of the Indus valley group is first seen, and in fact, it is with the Upanishads that the foundations of Hinduism were truly laid.

The law of karma was first put forth in the Upanishads. It gave hope to the servant caste, for even though they might be servants in this life, if they led charitable and humble lives they could be reborn into higher castes. The idea was also put forth in the Upanishads that if a man led several good lives he could escape the cycle of births and rebirths and unite with Brahman.

The Upanishads gave hope to the servant caste for only a short time, for soon most realized that they faced an endless cycle of rebirths. It would be practically impossible to go through several lifetimes without committing a sin that would cause a setback. The idea of striving throughout eternity, the soul never knowing peace or rest, was terrifying. At this time arose various sects, notably Buddhism, that rejected the authority of the priests in favor of individual reason about how to achieve peace. Buddhism and some of the other sects gained prominence in some of the Indian kingdoms for a while; however, Hinduism was not only a religion but a complete way of life and it had too firm a position to be driven out by other sects.

Hinduism gained additional strength when, beginning about 200 B.C., Indians went abroad and colonized Sumatra, Borneo, Java, Malaya, and Indochina. Colonization and the resulting missionary activity almost always brings new life to religion. Nonbelievers must be wooed into becoming believers. New cultures present new problems and new questions for the missionary religion to answer. New oral traditions must be created to explain the religion in ways the nonbelievers can understand.

The great epics of Hinduism were created at this time. All the deepest values of Hinduism, the individual's duties to himself and to society, are treated in warlike narratives and mythological scenes. The chief value of the epics was that they brought the teachings of the Upanishads to a level that the common man could understand. In contrast to the Vedas, "that which is heard," the epics and later sacred texts were known as "that which is remembered." Since they were not considered as sacred as the Vedas, which were forbidden to all but the three highest castes, they were open to all. The epics carried to the common people the message of the gods' love for all men, regardless of caste.

Hinduism now became more god-centered, and two gods, Vishnu and Siva, gained prominence over the older gods. Vishnu had been a minor god in earlier times, and Siva was probably a fertility god in the Indus valley religion at the time of the Aryan conquest. By now the universal spirit Brahman had been personified in the god Brahma, a remote and unapproachable god who created the universe and indeed was considered inseparable from it. The three gods were said to represent the three important functions of the Supreme— creation (Brahma), protection (Vishnu), and destruction (Siva)—and were known together as the Hindu Triad or Trinity. The power that was associated with each of these great gods was also later personified as his female companion.

The common people could feel close to these gods, could feel that the gods knew and cared about them. Devotion to a personal god developed, along with the practice of worshiping these personal gods with prayers, offerings, incense, or music. Images of these gods were made, temples were built to house them, and festivals and pilgrimages to places associated with the various gods became common.

The most important of the epics is the Bhagavad-Gita ("Song of the Lord"). It is a kind of sermon addressed to the hero, Arjuna, by Krishna, a fellow warrior, who reveals himself as none other than an incarnation of the Supreme Being. It was important because it laid the foundation for the idea of divine incarnations, which made it possible for gods worshiped in the form of animals and heroic men to become incarnations of Vishnu. It introduced a completely new aspect of Hinduism, the love of God for man and man for God. Here, for the first time, God separates Himself from the universe and meets man face to face on earth.

The epic ushered in what is considered the golden

age of Hinduism. During this time (A.D. 300–750) the majority of Hindus practiced a strongly personal and devotional religion. Fantastic stories and legends, called the Antiquities, were written in order to bring the traditional doctrines to the Hindu masses.

Female companions of the three gods of the Hindu Triad came into prominence as figures to be worshiped. The companion of Brahma, the creator, was called Sarasvati, the goddess of learning and knowledge. The companion of Vishnu, the protector, was called Lakshmi, the goddess of wealth and prosperity. And the destroyer Siva's companion was Sakti, the goddess of power. Sakti was above all a mother goddess, a development of the fertility goddesses who had been worshiped by the conquered peoples. Later, sects devoted to the worship of one or another of these gods and goddesses would arise.

With the increased availability of Hinduism to the masses came the revival of the more primitive practices of worship that had characterized the earlier religion. Among these were animal and sometimes human sacrifices, the burning of widows on their husbands' funeral pyres, and committing suicide in the name of the gods.

In the face of such excesses, many Hindus from the learned classes began to preach against these forms of worship. One philosopher and religious teacher named Sankara traveled all over India urging the people to cease the barbaric practices of widow-burning and sacrifice. He preached a return to the Vedas and Upanishads, and established four monasteries to continue his work. A man of great magnetism, Sankara was very successful, and today a majority of Hindus are Sankara's followers.

Medieval Hinduism

By the year 1000, the basic doctrines of Hinduism had been formed, and the ancient period of Hinduism gave way to the medieval period. The most important event of this period was the conquest of parts of India by the Muslims, whose religion, Islam, will be discussed in a later chapter. The Muslims considered it their sacred duty to convert the Hindus and in their zeal for saving souls often resorted to force, although many outcastes or untouchables converted voluntarily. Nevertheless, the Muslim conquest did not bring about any basic destruction of Hindu life and religion. Islam was absolutely alien to the Hindus; it challenged everything Hinduism had stood for throughout the centuries. In the face of this threat, and unable to assimilate the Muslims into its caste system as it had assimilated all previous invaders, Hinduism drew into itself. Rather than trying to fight the invaders, the Hindus decided instead to make their own religion stronger.

First in the south and then in the north, teachers and philosophers appeared, preaching love of God and absolute surrender to God as the quickest way to salvation. Many sects arose, and a mass of devotional poetry was written, in all the regional languages. It stressed simple faith and devotion to a personal god and urged brotherhood and friendship.

But by the end of the seventeenth century the devotional movement had lost much of its popularity, and the old ritualism and rigidity had begun to dominate Hinduism again. By the time British rule in India began, little life seemed to be left in Hinduism.

The Modern Period

The modern period of Hinduism began about 1800 with the introduction of British rule into India. These first European conquerors found a sterile religion with a thousand restrictions and customs looked upon as laws of God, including child marriage, no intermarriage between castes, the burning of widows, few rights for women, untouchability, and a ban on travel to foreign countries. It was such a rigid system that when the British broke the isolation of India and brought it into contact with European customs and ways, many Hindus, awed and excited by what seemed to be the complete freedom of British ways, began to imitate them. In fact, it was widely expected that India would become Christianized. But in the end, the threat of assimilation into Western culture revitalized Hinduism.

This revitalization was due to the work of several religious philosophers and poets, but it was Mohandas K. Gandhi (1869–1948), whose followers called him the Mahatma, or Great Soul, who is considered the greatest savior of the Hindus and of India. Gandhi saw that his country was slowly being destroyed by the British, who controlled all of India's natural resources and kept all the profits instead of using them to help the Indian people. He felt India must win its independence, but at the same time he realized that the Indian people would not unite against Britain, divided as they were by strong caste lines. He also realized that the Indians had not the arms or the power to fight the British by force.

Gandhi used the same technique against both the

caste system and the British—nonviolence. Non-violence had long been considered a virtue in Hinduism; it had been preached as one method that would help bring about rebirth into a higher caste. But in the past it had been applied only to individual action. Gandhi preached and practiced it as a collective action. According to Gandhi, truth is God, and nonviolence is the means of attaining truth. He developed a technique which he called "soul force," nonviolent defense of what one considers the truth.

In attacking the rigid lines of the caste system, Gandhi, born of a servant caste, organized the outcastes or untouchables in various towns and led them in nonviolent actions that crossed the rigid caste boundaries, such as using the well or road in a village that was taboo to them. The other castes countered violently, but under the leadership of Gandhi, the untouchables did not resist, willingly taking beatings and imprisonment. After all, they had nothing to lose. Eventually many in the higher castes could no longer justify their own violence in the face of the willing, even joyful manner in which the outcastes received it.

Against the British, Gandhi had to begin his nonviolent protest alone, for the Indians of the higher castes were fearful of jail and punishment by the British. In 1930 he began a "salt march" to the sea where he intended to make salt, an activity prohibited to anyone except the British. He was arrested and imprisoned, but he called for other Indians to continue his work. Gradually, the people began to answer his call. Within two years it was almost a disgrace for an Indian not to have been arrested and jailed for noncooperation with the British. Nevertheless, it took seventeen years of non-

violent protest and noncooperation before India se-
cured its independence from Great Britain.

Nearly all India had united against the British, but
many Hindus still resisted the abolishment of the caste
system. A year after independence Gandhi was assassi-
nated by a Hindu who believed in the established
Hindu doctrines and did not want to see them changed.
All his life Gandhi insisted he was a mortal man, but
most Indians worship him as a divine incarnation.

Ever since India gained its independence from Britain, its religious leaders have devoted great effort to
teaching the basic Hindu doctrines to the masses of
illiterate Indians. The Song of the Lord is widely read,
and most of the other great books have been published
in all the languages of India. The government has introduced many democratic reforms, with the result that
the caste system is slowly being abolished. However, it
is difficult to erase longstanding local customs, and
Harijans, or untouchables, still suffer unduly in many
rural areas of India. In 1989, more than 14,000 anti-
Harijan crimes or acts of discrimination were recorded
in India, and countless others probably went unre-
corded because the victims are afraid to report these
acts to the police. As India becomes industrialized, and
communication and education increase in the rural
areas, it is hoped that the caste system will die out
completely.

The sterile and ritualized Hinduism that the British
found when they first began to rule in India has been
discarded. In its place, the earliest form of Hinduism—
in which unity with Brahman, the universal spirit, is
the ultimate goal, and liberation from time, space, and
matter is the means to achieve that goal—is being re-

vived. In addition, Hinduism not only is enjoying renewed strength in India but also has gained much influence in the Western world. Beginning in the 1960s, Yoga, Indian mysticism, gurus (Hindu spiritual teachers), and the Hare Krishna cult became popular among youth in the United States and Western Europe. Hinduism, unlike Western religions, is an individual matter; it is a quest for liberation, a tendency to renounce material and worldly things, and an intensive concentration on problems which in other cultures are more often reserved for religious scholars and philosophers. All these elements attracted Western young people who rejected what they felt was the alienation, materialism, and worldliness of Western society.

One of the most famous gurus of the 1960s was the Maharishi Mahesh Yogi. Born in India, he was a student of Guru Dev, spiritual leader of northern India for 13 years. Five years after Dev's death, the Maharishi undertook a ten-year period of missionary work in the West. Based in California, he became a guru to many celebrities, including the Beatles, the Rolling Stones, and Mia Farrow, to whom he taught transcendental meditation. From the end of 1967 through 1968, he was the subject of cover stories in major magazines and was even a guest on "The Tonight Show" with Johnny Carson. Some critics called him a publicity-seeker, but his aim was to get his message to as many Westerners as he could. In 1968, at the end of his ten-year mission, he returned to India, where he attracts a substantial number of students from the West.

In the 1980s, the Baghwan Shree Rajneesh became as famous as the Maharishi Mahesh Yogi. He presided over an entire town in Oregon, called Rajneeshpuram, which was built by his American followers. He was forced to leave the United States in 1986 because of illegal immigration charges. Internal conflicts caused the followers he left behind to disperse.

The Hare Krishna movement is the best and most serious example of the adoption of the Hindu religion by young Westerners. It is a devotional movement dedicated to the service of God, or Krishna, the eternal, all-knowing, and all-powerful. It is based on the Bhagavad-Gita, or Song of the Lord, the Hindu epic written nearly two thousand years ago. The epic told of Krishna who, disguised as a warrior, revealed to fellow warrior Arjuna that he was an incarnation of the Supreme Being. It thus introduced into Hinduism the idea of the love of God for man and man for God.

The Hare Krishna movement is another name for the International Society for Krishna Consciousness. The society was founded by A. C. Bhaktivedanta Swami Prabhupada, who is looked to as a disciple of Buddha in an unbroken chain of spiritual teachers. In 1966 he came to the United States on the order of his spiritual master to preach to the people of the West.

The movement is simply a modern version of the devotional movements that have arisen in Hinduism throughout its history. Its basic belief is that people are born and live their lives without ever understanding who they are. Because of this "impure consciousness," a person is content to think of himself as a student or a parent or a businessman. But these are only temporary answers to the question "Who am I?" The devotees of Krishna Consciousness seek out "absolute truth," which they believe is contained in all the great scriptures of the world, in the Bible, the Torah, the Koran.

But the oldest known revealed scriptures are the Vedas, especially the Bhagavad-Gita, which is the record of God's actual words.

The "absolute truth" is that all people are servants of Krishna. Everyone has had countless births in the past and will have countless births in the future unless he can break away from birth and death by regaining his eternal status as a servant of Krishna. Understanding of the absolute truth qualifies one to enter Krishna's society, the spiritual kingdom that lies beyond the material universe.

The program offered by the International Society for Krishna Consciousness is designed so that each person may remain in his occupation or station of life. All he must do is perform simple devotional practices under the direction of a spiritual teacher and use whatever talents he has in the service of God. But whatever he does, twenty-four hours a day, he must do it with the consciousness that he is Krishna's eternal servant.

The easiest way for most people to achieve this consciousness is to chant the following bhajan, or devotional song: Hare Rama, Hare Rama, Rama Rama, Hare Hare, Hare Krishna, Hare Krishna, Krishna Krishna, Hare Hare. But this chant is not to be performed in privacy to gain salvation for oneself alone. The duty and obligation of the devotee is to go out into the streets where people can hear the chanting and see the dancing.

Even though the Hare Krishna movement in the United States reached its height in the 1960s and 1970s, one can still see in major cities young Americans dressed in saffron robes, the boys with shaved heads, the girls in braids or with their hair pulled back,

chanting the Hare Krishna and swaying to the music of
their bells and *mirdanga* drums. They can also be seen
in some major European cities as well as in Delhi, Hong
Kong, and Tokyo. But the Hare Krishna movement has
spread most quickly in the United States, where young
Americans have responded with great eagerness and
intensity. It is strange that so many converts have been
found in the United States and indeed in the West as a
whole, for the Hare Krishna movement's rejection of
individual identity, its strict regulations, etc., are so
basically Eastern. But for these young people, Western
religion and Western society have failed.

Hindu Religious Practices

Four definite sects exist in Hinduism today. Three of
them, Vaishnavism, Saivism, and Saktism, have existed
since ancient Hinduism. The fourth sect, called the
Smartas, consists of worshipers who do not belong to
these three sects but who follow the ancient traditions
and worship all the gods without distinction. The majority of Hindus do not belong to any sect, but their
religious practices do not differ basically from those of
other Hindus.

For all Hindus, religious activity centers chiefly in
the home. Each home has at least one image, idol, or
picture before which prayers, hymn singing, the offering of flowers, and the burning of incense are performed. The symbols used as objects of worship are, for
Vishnu, a fossilized ammonite shell taken from the
Gandake River; for Siva, a stone found in the Narmada
River; for Surya, the sun, a round marble stone. Wor-

ship may also be offered to books, as at the time of the festival devoted to Sarasvati, the goddess of learning.

Religious practices in the home involve worship three times daily: in the morning before dawn, any time after sunrise, and in the evening. Rituals always are preceded by bathing, and always involve prayers; offerings are made to the family deity and food is offered to animals and guests. No meal of any form can be taken in the household before the family deity is offered food.

Milestones in the individual's life are observed by rites, all requiring the help of a trained priest and a chaplain serving a family or group of families. At a birth the father or nearest male relative rubs the newborn's tongue with clarified butter and honey, sometimes also with powdered gold dust. Prayers for long life, intelligence, diligence, and concentration, but not for worldly gain, are offered.

The initiation is the most important ceremony, because it is the ceremony of entry into the Hindu religion. It is performed on adolescent boys only; females occupy a lowly place in the Hindu religion, although this, too, is changing in modern India. The boy is shaved and bathed, dressed in garments newly dyed with red chalk, a waist girdle of sacred grass, and a deerskin, and is provided with a staff. Prayers are offered on his behalf and he is given his first lessons in making offerings to the gods.

The marriage ceremony involves the worship of the bridegroom by the father of the bride. The bride is then given, with ornaments and presents for the groom. The groom accepts the hand of the bride and a fire offering is performed. The most important part of the ceremony is the Seven Steps, in which the bride and groom take seven steps around the fire, or go around the fire seven times. The ceremonies are begun with a formula of good intent (the bride and groom both wish a happy marriage) and ended by a prayer for peace.

The final sacrament is performed at death, ideally on the bank of a sacred river. Cremation occurs as soon after death as possible, accompanied by prayers. Some of the bones are thrown into the river or collected to be taken to a sacred river if there is none nearby. Monthly ceremonial prayers occur afterward, and at the end of the lunar year a ceremony is held at which the dead man is admitted to the company of his forefathers.

In the temples, trained ministrants perform regular ceremonies of worship—in the larger temples, several times a day. There is merit for a Hindu who attends these ceremonies alone or with his family, but he is not obligated to attend the temple, and congregational worship hardly exists in Hinduism. Much more important are the various methods of individual worship, especially meditation. Strengthened by yoga, meditation can lead to such a release of tension that the worshiper can accomplish the ultimate aim of union with Brahman, the Absolute.

At least once a year every important temple holds a festival. In the south of India these festivals always include a procession in which the god of the temple is pulled around the city or village on a cart or the back of an elephant. In the temple, dancing, singing, and the telling of religious stories goes on. Even festivals in small villages attract worshipers from far away who use them as the reason for pilgrimages. Pilgrimages, together with ceremonial baths in sacred rivers or temple tanks, are considered symbolic of the individual self's pilgrimage to the Supreme Spirit and its purification from all wrong deeds.

General days of festival are many, but only the more devout Hindus celebrate all of them. Probably the most commonly celebrated festivals occur in the autumn. The first ten days of the month Asin (September-October; Hindu months overlap those of the Western calendar) are especially sacred to Sakti, the mother goddess. For nine days she is worshiped in her destructive forms, and some sects sacrifice animals to her on the ninth day. The tenth day is celebrated by all sects with processions and merrymaking.

At the beginning of October-November, Diwali is celebrated. A New Year's festival, it is observed by the ceremonial lighting of lamps, the illuminating of house fronts, and the exchanging of presents.

Holi is a spring festival, occurring in February-March, which is dedicated to Krishna. During Holi, people celebrate the advent of spring by throwing colored water and powder on each other.

Many objects in nature are considered sacred in varying degrees, the most sacred being the cow. Worshiped as the representative of Mother Earth, the cow is divine in her own right, and the killing or eating of cows is forbidden in India. Among other sacred animals are bulls, monkeys, Indian tree squirrels, and snakes, which are especially associated with Siva. Two of the largest trees in India, the banyan and the pipal, are also sacred. All rivers and hills are to some extent divine, but the Ganges River is extremely holy, for it is believed to flow from the head of Siva. Any stream of water may symbolically stand for the sacred Ganges—even water poured from a jug.

In a limited sense, parents are divine to their children, as is the husband to the wife, the teacher to the student, tools to the worker, etc. Awareness of this divinity is not expressed through formal "worship" but simply through considerateness and respect.

Divinity is everywhere and all around every Hindu, and Westerners find such beliefs hard to understand. Yet the all-pervasiveness of divinity is the source of much of the dignity and humility of the Hindu culture—an attitude that many young Westerners have found attractive.

II

Buddhism

THERE IS SOME QUESTION WHETHER BUDDHISM, AT least in its original form, is a religion at all. The Fathers of the Buddhist church reject all ideas of a Supreme Being or of a soul or self that is a reflection of the Divine. Instead, Buddhism has been called a discipline.

Buddhism was founded by Gautama Buddha, chiefly as a reaction to some of the doctrines of Hinduism. Buddha seems to have believed in transmigration of souls and the law of karma, in gods and evil spirits, and in the cycle of births and rebirths. He departed from Hindu doctrine in teaching that the cycle of births and rebirths could be broken, did not have to be lived out. Breaking the cycle was a difficult task, but it could be done if one attained correct knowledge and the discipline to take advantage of that knowledge. Each one

23

must work out his own enlightenment, although others might help him. The correct knowledge to be obtained was that desires for pleasure, wealth, long life, and so forth, were what caused one to be reborn. The discipline that would enable one to take advantage of that knowledge was the loss of all such earthly desires.

The goal is *nirvana*, which Buddha defined as the end of desire. It also meant freedom, inward peace, and joy, a state in which birth, age, sickness, pain, and death ceased.

At times in history, particularly in the East but also sometimes in the West, the Buddhist way has enjoyed great popularity, and Gautama Buddha is counted among men like Jesus Christ and Muhammad as one of the most influential figures in human history.

The Life of Buddha

There is little question that Guatama Buddha really existed, but like those of other legendary figures the actual events of his life are shadowy. This is due partly to the mythology that has grown up around his life and partly to the fact that his life was not recounted in writing until several generations after his death. Probably the main course of his life and chief teachings have been accurately preserved.

Gautama Buddha's parents, Maha Maya and Suddhodana, belonged to the ruling house of the Sakya clan. Suddhodana reigned over Kapilavastu, a small village on the Indian slope of the Himalayas. There, about 560 B.C., a son was born to Maha Maya.

According to Buddhist legend, this was no ordinary

birth. The child was conceived by Maha Maya in a dream. She dreamed that she was miraculously transported away to the mountains where she bathed in a beautiful lake and then lay down upon a couch in a golden mansion on a silver hill. Then a beautiful white elephant carrying a white lotus flower in his trunk approached from the north and entered her womb. At that moment the heavens and the earth gave forth signs; the earth was covered with lotus flowers and lotuses fell from the sky. The mute spoke and the lame walked.

Maha Maya told the Brahmans of her dream, and they told her it meant she had conceived a son who would become a universal monarch if he adopted the life of a householder; but if he adopted the religious life he would remove ignorance and sin from the world.

The boy was named Siddhartha ("he who has realized his goal"). He also received the family name Gautama and the clan name Sakyamuni. Maha Maya died seven days after Siddhartha's birth, and the boy was brought up in his father's house by his aunt Maha Pajapati.

Siddhartha's father adored him and vowed that his son would experience no unhappiness, banning all sight of human suffering from his court and ordering that his son be shielded from all unpleasant sights when he left the palace. In this happy, protected environment Siddhartha developed great intelligence. And his physical strength was so great that at the age of sixteen, in an archery contest, he shot an arrow through seven trees and won the right to marry his cousin Yashodara.

It was not until several years later that Siddhartha learned that the happy world in which he had always lived was not at all like the real world. Four times in a row, as he rode in his chariot through the town to the pleasure gardens, he received this revelation. The first time he saw an old man, the second time a sick man, the third time a dead man, and the fourth, a beggar monk. At the sight of the first three, Siddhartha was overwhelmed. If earthly existence contained such sorrows, what was the use of living? But he took heart in the calmness and serenity of the beggar monk and decided that the best way to escape sorrow was to become a beggar monk himself.

Siddhartha returned from his fourth trip to the pleasure gardens determined to set out immediately as a beggar monk. But when he arrived at home, he found that his wife had given birth to a son, Rahula, and instead of feeling happiness upon hearing the news Sidhartha was filled with despair. Now he was a father with great responsibilities; he would be bound to the life of a householder.

But Siddhartha's desire to become a beggar monk was stronger than his desire not to shirk his responsibilities. One night he secretly left his wife and infant son, called for his horse Kanthaka and his charioteer Chandaha, and rode to the woods. There he exchanged his silk robes for a suit of bark and sent back his horse and charioteer, who died of grief at their master's departure. Siddhartha began a new life.

For six years Siddhartha sought a life of communion with Brahman, listening to the teachings of Brahman beggar monks, fasting, and going without other physical comforts. To further his concentration upon spiritual things, Siddhartha did not sit but rested crouched upon his heels. His bed was made of brambles, and often only a single grain of rice was his food for the day. But although his body became little but skin and bones and although he went through every form of self-torture imaginable, he still did not achieve enlightenment, the understanding of human existence, and escape from sorrow.

While growing up, Siddhartha had experienced every comfort of life and had been deprived of nothing. After he had left his family, he had experienced every hardship and discomfort. Neither way of life had brought him enlightenment, and it was the realization of this truth that caused him to understand "the middle way." Either extreme meant desires and strivings, trying through passions and pleasures or through pain and suffering to become something that he was not. Neither could lead to peace and understanding. Only the rejection of desires, pleasure, and pain—the middle way—could bring enlightenment.

Siddhartha began to go to the villages to beg food to restore his strength. His five traveling companions, who continued to believe that hardship and rejection of comfort was the only path to enlightenment, left Siddhartha, and he now traveled alone.

One day he arrived near the village of Uruvella and sat down under a banyan tree by a river to wait for the hour when it was proper to go into the village and beg. Sujata, a farmer's daughter who had made a vow to carry an annual offering to the spirit of the banyan tree, brought her offering that day in the form of a golden bowl full of goat's milk curds. When she saw Siddhartha under the tree, she thought he was the spirit in human form and gave the bowl to him. He drank the goat's milk curds and then threw the bowl into the river. But miraculously, instead of floating downstream with the current, the bowl floated upstream! Siddhartha realized that this was a sign, and he resolved to remain by the river until he had attained supreme enlightenment.

Legend has it that Mara (the Buddhist devil) saw that Siddhartha was near to achieving enlightenment, and he was furious. He led an army of demons to attack Siddhartha with darkness, fire, and a rain of rocks, sand, and ashes. It was so violent that all the friendly gods fled, leaving Siddhartha to fight for himself. But Siddhartha was untouched; all these missiles only fell like a rain of heavenly flowers or hung in the air like a canopy over his head. Then Mara tried to tempt Siddhartha, offering him the lordship of the earth and every kind of earthly pleasure. But Siddhartha was unmoved. Seeing Mara and his demons powerless against Siddhartha, the friendly gods returned and honored him, and that night Siddhartha sank into the deepest thought he had ever known and by morning he had attained supreme enlightenment. He became Buddha, the Enlightened One.

In Buddhism, not everyone who attains enlightenment becomes a Buddha. A Buddha is one who attains supreme enlightenment, a goal that takes many lives and much helping of others before it is attained. According to Buddhist legend, Siddhartha was actually a man named Sumedha reborn. Countless ages before, Sumedha had attained enlightenment but had put off entering nirvana in order to help other men gain enlightenment. His life as Siddhartha would be his final life, for in it he would attain supreme enlightenment and would enter nirvana at his death. Thus, when, as Siddhartha, he attained supreme enlightenment, he became a Buddha.

Buddha now faced a decision: should he preach his truth to others? At first he doubted that his efforts would do any good. Attaining the truth had been a long and difficult task for him and he did not feel willing to reveal the truth to men who were filled with desire and hatred and who would be blind to it. But at last he decided to try to help them.

Buddha knew that the five men who had been his companions while he had been an ascetic were now living in the Deer Park at Isipatana in Benares, and he decided to go there and preach the truth to them.

The words Buddha spoke in the Deer Park to the five men who had been his companions were the first he spoke to others as Buddha, and they have become basic to all Buddhist literature. His first sermon came to be called "Setting in Motion the Wheel of the Law." In it he spoke of the two extremes which he himself had experienced and advised that neither should be followed. Instead, he said, a middle path existed which would lead to understanding and peace and higher wisdom: in other words, to nirvana. He then presented what he called the Four Noble Truths and the Eightfold Path to Enlightenment.

The Four Noble Truths are: (1) Existence contains suffering. (2) The cause of suffering is thirst or desire for pleasure, prosperity, and continued life. It is this thirst and desire that cause one to be reborn. (3) The way to escape from suffering and continued rebirth is to rid oneself of desire. (4) To be freed from desire, one

must follow the Eightfold Path: right views; right aspi-
rations; right speech, conduct, and mode of livelihood;
right effort; right mindfulness; and right rapture.

When they heard Buddha's sermon, the five monks
were converted, and within the next four days all five
had attained the goal of the first path. On the fifth day,
Buddha preached a second sermon, called "On the
Non-Existence of Soul," in which he told them that
nothing—not the body or feelings or senses—was permanent. The realization of the impermanence of all
these things. Buddha continued, would cause one to
lose all his desires and become free. After all, if nothing
was permanent, then nothing was worth desiring and
striving after. The man who realized this would not
desire to be reborn into a higher caste and thus would
escape the infernal cycle of rebirth and attain nirvana.

For Buddha, nirvana did not mean a uniting of the
individual soul with the universal soul; it did not mean
the same thing as Brahman in Hinduism. Instead, it
meant the end of rebirths, or "extinction," and Buddha
explained it by the example of a lamp that goes out
because of lack of fuel. If a man no longer fans the
flames of passion, it is extinguished. Like the lamp
which, when extinguished, no longer has a flame, a
man whose life no longer burns in a flame of passion is
not reborn again. For most men, such a process took
several lives, Buddha taught.

After this second sermon, the five monks attained
enlightenment. The next day, a young man named Yasa
and fifty-four companions, who were also resting in the
Deer Park, did so as well. There were then sixty persons
besides Buddha who knew the truth. He sent them out
in different directions to spread the message. Buddha

then went to preach in Uruvella and Rajagantha, where he gained many more followers.

Many indians were ripe for Buddha's message, since Hinduism had ceased to hold any hope for them. It will be remembered from the last chapter that in the sixth and fifth centuries B.C., when Buddhism arose, Hindu society had become very rigid. Lines of caste were becoming fixed; ritualism and the social dominance of the Brahman (priest) caste prevailed. Indian thought was characterized by fear of eternal reincarnation and fear of the soul's inability to escape earthly life. Buddha preached that the loss of those very fears could lead to escape from earthly life and eternal reincarnation, and that a man could accomplish this no matter what caste he belonged to. There was no need for the leadership of the Brahmans, either as priests or as experts in religious ritual. In a way, Buddhism was a revolt against the Brahmans. Eight months after he attained enlightenment, Buddha had twenty thousand followers.

Then, accompanied by all twenty thousand, Buddha returned to his home, Kapilavastu, to carry his message to the Sakya clan. Within a short time many of the Sakya men, including Buddha's father, Suddhodana, had begun along the path to enlightenment. Buddha's son, Rahula, was also accepted as one of his followers. Rahula went with Buddha when he took leave of his family and Kapilavastu and began the life of wandering that he was to lead until the end of his days.

For nine months of the year Buddha and the three hundred to five hundred disciples who traveled with him wandered through the countryside, acting not as priests but as teachers of the way of enlightenment through the example of their lives. During the three months of the rainy season they settled outside a town, sufficiently far away so that they could meditate, but close enough to beg for food. There the disciples waited on Buddha and listened to his teachings, and people from near and far also came to hear his words.

Together, Buddha's disciples were called the Community. It was open to all, regardless of caste, for Buddha taught that nirvana could be reached by all who conformed to the strict rules of the monastic life. He did not seek to bring about an end to the caste system itself, though, for he thought the system was necessary for the structuring of earthly life. All the beggar monks wore yellow robes and were absolutely forbidden to destroy life, steal, lie, commit unchaste or other impure acts, drink strong drinks, dance or sing or act in any public shows, ornament themselves, receive money, eat between meals, or use high or luxurious beds. The rules forbidding these ten things are sometimes called the Ten Commandments of Buddhism.

Gradually, there grew up a laity composed of men who followed the teachings of Buddha as much as they could while continuing to lead their lives in the villages. As their number increased, Buddha gave permission for them to attach themselves to the order. These laymen were eager to support the monks, helping them to get food and shelter, and the monks were unable to do without their help. In return for this help and for obeying the first five prohibitions, the laymen were promised certain heavenly rewards, including rebirth as beggar monks. Nirvana was never promised as a reward, for only total renunciation of the world could lead to deliverance.

In the fifth year after the Enlightenment, Buddha

received word that his father was dying. He went immediately to Kapilavastu in order to help his father achieve enlightenment, and because of his efforts, Suddhodana attained the fourth path and reached nirvana before he died. Buddha's aunt, Maha Pajapati, now decided to adopt the monastic life. She cut off her hair and, accompanied by the wives of the Kapilavastu men who had become disciples of Buddha when he had visited the village, went to the place where Buddha was staying. She told him that now that Suddhodana was dead and the other women's husbands were gone, she and they wished to retire from the world and to be admitted into the Community. But Buddha refused, and when he was asked twice more, he refused twice more.

Women occupied a very subservient role in Indian society, and Buddha's opinion of women's role in earthly society conformed to the general view. But in the face of Maha Pajapati's pleas he finally relented, and women were admitted into the Community as nuns under the condition that they be totally subordinate to the monks. But, he stated, because women had been admitted, the truth he preached, the Good Law, would last for only five hundred years, while it would have endured for one thousand years if women had not been admitted.

Buddha and his disciples wandered for many years, and during these years Buddhist legend recounts many exciting and tragic events. An attempt was made on Buddha's life, his doctrines were opposed by many dissenting sects, some of his own followers proved disloyal to him, and he received the news that almost the entire Sakya clan had been destroyed in a war.

Through all this, Buddha remained intent upon his goal of spreading his message, and the number of his followers increased every year.

After twenty years of wandering Buddha chose the disciple Ananda to be his permanent attendant, which meant that Ananda brought his water and tooth twig, washed his feet, accompanied him on journeys, carried his bowl and cloak, and swept his cell. Ananda had not even attained enlightenment and indeed would not until after Buddha's death, but Buddha had recognized great wisdom and humility in Ananda, and among the monks the young man came to be known as "the venerable Ananda."

When he was seventy-nine years old and had been preaching for over forty-five years, Buddha became very ill, and it was clear that he would not live much longer. When he was well enough to talk, Ananda asked him what instructions he planned to leave for his disciples, and Buddha answered that he did not intend to leave any instructions. The Community was not dependent upon him, he said, and should be able to carry on without his help after his death.

He went on: "Therefore, O Ananda, be ye lamps unto yourselves. Be ye a refuge to yourselves. Betake yourselves to no external refuge. Hold fast as a refuge to the Truth. Look not for refuge to anyone besides yourselves. . . . And whosoever, Ananda, either now or after I am dead, shall be a lamp unto themselves, shall betake themselves to no external refuge . . . shall look not for refuge to anyone besides themselves—it is they, Ananda, among my Bhikkus [Brethren] who shall reach the very topmost Height!—but they must be anxious to learn."

Soon after this conversation took place, Buddha called together all the brethren and announced to them that in three months' time he would die. He then went to the mango grove of Cunda, a blacksmith, and instructed Cunda in the truth. Cunda was grateful and invited Buddha to dine at his house.

After eating the meal, Buddha became very sick, and he knew death was near. He summoned Ananda and told him that Cunda should not be blamed for serving him his last meal, he would be reborn to a long life of fortune and fame. Buddha also instructed Ananda not to grieve over his death, for "the spirits who are free from passion bear it calm and self-possessed, mindful of the saying, 'Impermanent, indeed, are all component things.'" He then commanded Ananda to call all the brethren so that he could speak to them. His last words before he died were: "Decay is inherent in all component things! Work out your salvation with diligence!" Then Buddha entered nirvana. According to most scholars, this was about 480 B.C.

When Buddha was taken sick the first time, Ananda had asked what was to be done with his remains, and Buddha had simply told him not to honor them. But after Buddha's death, his body was burned, and the teeth, clothing, and pieces of bone were divided among all those who laid claim to them: among those, the rulers of the various villages and kingdoms where important events in the life of Buddha had occurred. In the end, ten monuments were built for Buddha, including one for the vessel that had held the ashes and another for the ashes themselves. A whole town was built around the monument that held the hair that Buddha had given one of his disciples.

Soon, pilgrimages were being made to the places where the principal events of Buddha's life had occurred: Kapilavastu, his birthplace; Bodh Gaya, where he acquired supreme enlightenment; Sarnath, near Benares, where he set in motion the Wheel of the Law; and Kusinara, where he entered perfect nirvana. It is doubtful that Buddha would have approved of these practices and certain that he would not have approved what was done with his remains. But in later Buddhist writings Buddha is said to have ordered both practices.

Buddha had not believed in a strong religious framework or spiritual authority, and his refusal to establish such a framework before his death caused grave consequences for Buddhism as he had taught it. Without his leadership, the Community soon found itself threatened by divisions. Perhaps because of this unhappy state of affairs within the Buddhist ranks, Buddha's faithful servant, Ananda, who had attained enlightenment after Buddha's death, wrote down the parables, discourses, and sermons of the master. But despite this and other efforts to prevent the Community from breaking up, by the time one hundred years had passed after the death of Buddha, definite divisions existed. The chief division was between the School of the Elders, which held strictly to doctrine and practice as originally taught by Buddha, and the Great Community, which interpreted doctrine and practice with greater freedom, chiefly so that Buddhism would appeal to more people. As groups of monks multiplied and spread to different parts of India, other divisions occurred. Buddhism was fast disintegrating.

Then in the third century B.C., Buddhism, or at least that of the Elders, received much-needed assistance from the emperor Asoka. Asoka, whose empire joined the basins of the Ganges and Indus rivers, began his reign by waging wars of conquest. But when he realized the horrors that these wars caused, he vowed to devote himself to a life of good deeds. Attracted by the gentleness and compassion of Buddhism, he dedicated his life to spreading the Buddhist doctrine, not only among his own subjects but also among the people of neighboring states.

Through Asoka's missionaries, Buddhism was adopted in Ceylon and Burma; attracted many believers in northwest India, Kashmir, and Afghanistan; and even reached the Greek kingdoms of the Mediterranean. Clearly, Buddhism was on the way to becoming a universal religion. Asoka was also responsible for the establishment of a definite *dharma*, or code of ethics, for his subjects—a code of ethics that was adopted by much of the Buddhist world.

The Two Great Branches of Buddhism

By the first century B.C., the various schools and divisions within Buddhism had shaped themselves into two large schools or branches: Hinayana (Little Vehicle) and Mahayana (Great Vehicle). *Yana* means "vehicle," and it is through yana that the Buddhist crosses the river of rebirth and arrives upon the shore of nirvana.

"Little Vehicle" is a derisive name given by the followers of the Great Vehicle to those who insisted on holding to the original Buddhist doctrine and did not attempt to elaborate and embroider upon it so that it would appeal to the masses. This branch is actually the original School of the Elders, and because it strictly follows the doctrine of Buddha it needs little additional explanation. Its chief additions to Buddhism have been in the form of literature, beginning with the parables, discourses, and sermons of Buddha written down by Ananda, later including the rules of the Community and how they were formulated, and much later including a collection of commentaries on doctrine.

The Great Vehicle is actually the original Great Community. The major reason for the growth of the Great Vehicle was that Buddhism in its original form, or as taught by Buddha, was too narrow and too difficult for common people to practice. Even in the time of Buddha the laity was separated from and largely ignored by the monks and did not have a feeling of true membership in the religion. In order to give the laity a greater feeling of inclusion, some monks felt that Buddhist doctrine should be expanded.

The teachers of the Great Vehicle did not reject the old Buddhist doctrine but simply declared that it was incomplete. The written tradition was only a part of Buddha's teaching, and only a part was given to the Indian people because they were not yet ready to understand the wisdom in all its fullness. They first had been able to understand only the simpler principles of the Little Vehicle and to seek as their reward nirvana alone. But now Buddha had revealed to them that divine knowledge ought to be theirs and that they should become Buddhas like himself, putting off entering nirvana in order to help others who are still struggling to attain enlightenment.

While the supreme aim of original and Hinayana

Buddhism is personal escape from the dreadful cycle of rebirth, the supreme aim of Mahayana Buddhism is to help one's fellowman to attain deliverance. The ideal is not the Arahat, who wishes only his own nirvana, but the Bodhisattva, who upon the threshold of nirvana refuses to enter and chooses instead to stay in the temporal world helping others. After several lifetimes the Bodhisattva attains supreme enlightenment, becomes a Buddha, and upon his death finally enters nirvana.

Although Hinayanists denounced the Mahayanist concept of Boddhisatvas, the concept was already present in their own teachings. Gautama Buddha, after he had attained supreme enlightenment, himself resisted entering nirvana immediately and chose instead to spend long years wandering and teaching. Mahayanists simply extended the concept.

The Great Vehicle also expanded on the idea of worship of Buddha. During Buddha's lifetime, a man could prove he was a Buddhist by reciting the Triple Refuge formula: "I take refuge in the Buddha. I take refuge in the Law preached by the Buddha. I take refuge in the Order!" After Buddha's death, the formula had to mean that in some way he still existed and that some relationship could be established between him and the worshiper. Early Buddhism had avoided all images of Buddha himself, but with the growth of the Great Vehicle thousands of statutes of Buddha appeared, an idolatry that Buddha would have condemned.

Eventually the doctrine of the three bodies of Buddha evolved. He possessed a "body of creation" as long as he traveled upon earth and engaged in human activity there; a "body of delight" when he entered heavenly regions; and a "body of law" when he joined with the Absolute, the basis and source of all being.

The Mahayanists applied this doctrine not just to Gautama Buddha but to all Buddhas. The Little Vehicle had very early maintained that the Buddha had been preceded by other Buddhas but had not been much concerned with these predecessors. In the Great Vehicle so much emphasis is put upon other Buddhas and Bodhisattvas that Gautama Buddha has been pushed into second place.

With the Great Vehicle, Buddhism becomes a popular religion—appealing to the most scholarly thinker and the most illiterate worshiper alike. The chief reason for its success is that it abandoned the atheism of original Buddhism. This atheism could not long satisfy the human spirit in need of knowledge of a higher Being able to change the cause and effect of the law of karma (the process by which acts in one life determine the life into which a person is reborn). Mahayana Buddhism substituted ideas of paradise and hell much like those of Western religions. The Great Vehicle almost completely erases the original character of Buddhism.

Later History of Buddhism

Through the missionary activity of Asoka, Buddhism spread across the entire Indian subcontinent and by about the fifth century it had achieved the height of its influence. Much of this influence was due to the liberalism of the Mahayanist doctrine, which generously welcomed and included popular Indian beliefs. But Buddhism was never a serious threat to Hinduism. Hinduism was supported by the caste system and powerful with the authority of the Vedas, while Buddhism stood outside the active life and ignored the sacred tradition of India.

From the beginning of the ninth century, Buddhism no longer flourished except in those districts where it had been declared a state religion. But it was in the twelfth century, with the Muslim invasion, that the Indian career of Buddhism was truly ended. It had extended over nearly fifteen centuries, far exceeding Gautama Buddha's most optimistic prediction of one thousand years. But now it was truly over. By 1971 not even one percent of Indians were Buddhists. Nevertheless, Buddhism was destined to prosper in nearly all the countries of the Far East.

Buddhism was introduced to southern Asia, first in Ceylon and Burma, as a result of Asoka's missionary activity. Later it spread to Thailand, Cambodia, and Laos. From Ceylon and Burma, it spread to China, and from there to Korea and from Korea to Japan. It entered Tibet from either China or India. Buddhism fared better in some of these countries than in others, and although it exists in all of these countries and more, it is the official religion only in Cambodia, Japan, and Tibet. Although both Hinayana and Mahayana Buddhism exist in nearly all these countries, Hinayana is found chiefly in Ceylon, Burma, and Thailand, while Mahayana predominates in China, Tibet, Mongolia, Korea, and Japan.

Tibetan Buddhism is called Lamaism. (*Lama* was originally an honorary title given to very holy monks, although now every Tibetan monk is a lama.) Lamaism believes in the literal reincarnation of Buddhas and Bodhisattvas, and thus when a lama who is thought to be a divine incarnation dies, Tibetans immediately begin to look for the child into whose body the lama's soul has passed. The child is discovered by means of some event at his birth or some miracle he has performed and is taken before the members of the religious order of the late Buddha, where he is required to identify objects belonging to the late Buddha and otherwise to prove himself. Once he has done so, he is immediately raised to the dignity of the deceased lama.

It is in Tibet that Buddhism has achieved its greatest triumph. One out of every five Tibetan men dedicates himself to the monastic life. But Tibetan Buddhism is based on an offshoot of Mahayana that emphasizes the supernatural and sacred rites directed toward pure magic. To this the Tibetans have added their own magic rites and sorcery, their own religion, Bon.

It permeates the whole life of the people and is not only their religion but also their government. Until the middle of this century, the Dalai Lama, head of the church, also ruled the state. Then, in 1950, Communist Chinese occupied Tibet from the north. The fourteenth Dalai Lama, Bstandzin-rgya-mtsho, who had been enthroned in 1940 at the age of five, was then a teenager. The Chinese allowed him to remain in his position as a means of controlling the conquered territory. In 1959, however, the Tibetan people staged an unsuccessful revolt against the Communists, and the Dalai Lama fled into exile in India, which granted asylum to him and large numbers of other Tibetans. In 1990 the Dalai Lama remained in exile, but in spite of the physical absence of their leader and of the official atheism of Chinese Communism, Buddhism continues to thrive in Tibet.

Buddhism in Mongolia, another neighbor of China,

has also survived extinction under Communism, in this case Soviet Communism. Influenced by the Russian revolution, Communists in Mongolia took control of the country in 1921 and brought it under the Soviet umbrella, although it remained independent. At the time, Mongolia had some 120,000 lamas, nearly half of the male population. After the Communist revolution, all but one of the Buddhist monasteries were closed down. The lamas continued to practice their religion in private, and when the democratization movement began to spread through the Soviet bloc in the 1980s, the public practice of Buddhism quickly re-emerged. By 1990 the monasteries were open again and bustling with activity.

In Japan, Buddhism arrived late but took hold very quickly, in terms of historical time. It arrived from China via Korea around 550 A.D., and by the seventh century every Japanese house was supposed to have a Buddhist altar. Japan already had a traditional religion, Shinto, or The Way of the Gods, and Shinto is still practiced in Japan today. But it is mostly concerned with earthly life, does not look beyond death, and does not imagine a higher state of consciousness. The Japanese responded to the Buddhist ideas of reincarnation and karma and enlightenment.

They were even more attracted to a type of Buddhism that was introduced from China in the twelfth century. Called Chan in China, it was known as Zen in Japan. This type of Mahayana Buddhism easily combined with other religions, like Taoism in China. In Japan, Zen Buddhist monks said that the chief Shinto gods were manifestations of former Buddhas. Buddhist priests moved into Shinto shrines and took part in in

Shinto festivals. Because Shinto did not deal with death, Buddhists took charge of all activities surrounding death.

Zen is known as the "sudden school" of Buddhism because a major doctrine is that every living creature possesses the Buddha nature, or the Spirit which unites all things, and need only realize the great truth of life. That is not to say that Zen offers a shortcut to enlightenment. Years of discipline and meditation are required before the realization of the oneness of all things can take place. Zen does not rely on books or study, but the teacher is very important. It is the teacher who shakes the student out of the customary channel of thoughts by asking questions in the form of riddles which make the student ponder the nature of things. An example of such a riddle is "What is the sound of one hand clapping?"

Several early attempts were made to extend Buddhism into the West. The Emperor Asoka had sent missionaries as far as the Greek kingdoms of Syria, Egypt, Cyrene, and even Macedonia. Some scholars say that Buddhism reached as far into Egypt as those regions where Christianity was born and that Buddhist influence can be detected in the Gospels of St. Mark and St. John. Also, some Buddhists state that Gautama Buddha, under the name of Josaphat (derived from Bodhisattva, and indeed the name of an Indian prince who was converted to Christianity following experiences resembling those of the true Buddha), was able to enter the souls of a number of Christian saints. The Christian Church strongly denies all such speculations.

But the career of Buddhism in the West, unlike that in the East, was practically nonexistent. Some scholars suggest that the reason for this failure was the collapse of the Roman Empire and the triumph of Christianity; the resulting barrier that existed between India and Europe prevented all contact until the discovery of a sea route to the East Indies in 1498. But most agree that the chief reason is the deep incompatibility between Eastern and Western thought. While the West is rich materially, it is very poor spiritually. In contrast, the East is poor materially but rich in spiritual existence.

It was not until the nineteenth century that European thinkers began to study Buddhism, but they gave it more attention than other Indian philosophies. In England, a Roman Catholic monk named Thomas Merton wrote extensively on Zen and died in Asia searching for Zen sources. In the United States, a former Episcopal minister named Allan Watts also studied and wrote widely on Zen. Some scholars have discerned a pattern to the times when Westerners renew their interest in Eastern religions. Two such times have been after World War I, which was seen by many European thinkers as the final failure of Western religion, and in the 1960s and 70s when the young, particularly, rejected the materialism and violence of Western society. Perhaps it is true that when the burdens of science and technology become too great, the Western world turns to the simple spirituality of the East.

Modern Buddhist Practices

In countries where Hinayana Buddhism is practiced, a close relationship exists between the monks and the laity, although the laity do not belong to the order as the

laity in the West belong to churches. In these countries
the order is made up of practicing monks who have
taken vows, wear the yellow robe, and live the monastic
life. Yet except in Ceylon, where a monk's ordination is
for life, laymen become part of the Community for a
few weeks, months, or years, and then return to the
worldly life when they choose to.

While a man is in the monastery, his life is regulated
by the rules laid down in the Hinayana doctrine. He
must remain pure in thought and deed and observe
silence in his begging rounds. His only personal pos-
sessions are one undergarment, two yellow robes, a
belt, an alms bowl, a small knife or razor, a needle, and
a water strainer. Everything else is the common property of the Community.

Lay followers in the Hinayana countries look to the
monks for instruction in right living. This is given in
popular sermon form, with examples drawn from stories of the Buddha's previous rebirths. Right living in-
cludes reciting the Triple Refuge formula and
abstaining from killing, stealing, unlawful sexual inter-
course, bad speech, and liquor. Appropriate duties are
urged between parents and children, teachers and students, husbands and wives, friends and companions,
masters and servants, monks and lay people. Devout
followers maintain small shrines in their homes, go to
preaching halls to hear doctrine, and, if possible, go on
pilgrimages to sacred sites in India, Ceylon, Burma, or
Thailand. With the aid of monks, the people observe
ceremonies when a child reaches puberty, attend the
ordination ceremony when a young man enters the
order, and carry out burial rites.

Of the religious festivals, the chief is Wesak (usually

in May) which commemorates the triple events of the Buddha's birth, enlightenment, and death. Another is the feast of the offering of robes and alms to the monks at the end of the rainy season. Especially happy is the New Year's festival with its many amusements, processions, and dances, as well as the paying of honors to Buddha. There are also special local festivals.

Practices are much more varied in Mahayana countries, although their basic outlines and organization are similar to Hinayanist ones. Depending upon the country and the sect, the laity participate in traditional rituals in large measure or hardly at all. There are many more rituals because more Buddhas and Bodhisattvas are worshiped. Social service is stressed more in Mahayanist countries and is less personal than in Hinayanist countries. While in Hinayana countries the layman goes to the monks for help, Mahayana Buddhists actively offer their help to the laity and spend much time building orphanages, hospitals, and schools. This is because they are motivated by the Bodhisattva spirit.

The treatment of images in Mahayana countries is more complex than in Hinayana countries, for although Hinayanists worship images of Gautama Buddha, Mahayanists worship images of numerous Buddhas and Bodhisattvas. Most Hinayanists view the images as aids to meditation on the virtue of the Buddha. In Mahayanist countries, especially China and Tibet, images are more often prized as miraculous or supernatural, and acts performed in their presence are magically potent.

There are also many more festivals. In addition to those observed by the Hinayanists, there are festivals devoted to the various Buddhas and Bodhisattvas whom the Mahayanists worship.

For all Buddhists, meditation and Yoga are the chief forms of individual everyday worship. Both are means of transcending earthly life and achieving union, however temporary, with the higher wisdom. Important also are pilgrimages to the reliquaries containing the remains of the Buddha.

Treasured relics vary. Where a particular one is honored in a special sanctuary, such as the Temple of the Sacred Tooth in Ceylon, worship services are held daily. Objects made sacred by association are the banyan tree, or its descendant, at Bodh Gaya, under which Gautama experienced his great enlightenment; shoots from this same tree planted elsewhere; footprints of the Buddha; his girdle, alms bowl, etc. These, together with mementos of noted disciples and Arahats, have long played a role in popular devotion. As in other world religions, the remaining objects of lives that have been close to the first truth are important for the faith of those who have followed. Without a strong, central authority, Buddhist practices have diverged greatly over the centuries, but in the last half of the twentieth century modern means of communication and transportation have made it possible for representatives of many different schools of Buddhist thought to come together for the first time in history in a series of Buddhist Ecumenical Councils. Working together, Buddhists hope to achieve renewed growth.

III

Judaism

AT FIRST THE RELIGION OF A SMALL GROUP OF PEOPLE, Judaism has become a universal religion, and belief in its God, more than in any other, has reached the ends of the earth. For the God of Israel is also the God of Christendom and the God of Islam; and Judaism is the source of these other two great religions.

The word *Judaism* comes from the Hebrew word *Yehudah* which means "(The) Praised." Yehudah, or Judah, was the founder of a tribe and his name became the name of the tribe. From the name of a tribe it became the name of a kingdom and finally the name of a new state. Now the word *Judaism* is used to describe not simply a religion but the union of a God, a people (Israel), and a country (the Holy Land). In fact, it is impossible to separate the three elements from one another; the story of Judaism is the story of the Jews'

49

relationship with God and with the Holy Land. It is a story that goes back nearly four thousand years.

The History of Judaism

The Period Before Exile

The history of Israel and of Judaism begins about 2000 B.C. with Abraham, who is said to have been born in Ur, a center of advanced civilization in what was then Chaldea, in Egypt. Ur was a great center of the worship of the moon, and Abraham was brought up to worship the moon and other nature gods. But gradually Abraham came to feel that there was really only one God, the maker of all things, and thus he broke with the idol-worship of his family and community. According to the Old Testament, Abraham was rewarded for his wisdom when he was ninety-nine years old, for the Lord appeared to him and said: "I am God Almighty; walk before me, and be blameless. And I will make my covenant between me and you, and will multiply you exceedingly. . . . And I will give to you, and to your descendants after you, the land of your sojournings, all the land of Canaan, for an everlasting possession; and I will be their God". Abraham left his family and his country and, gaining converts to his new faith along the way, traveled west to Canaan. In Canaan, the Lord entered into a covenant with Abraham, promising to give the land to his descendants and to make them a chosen people as an example to the other peoples of the world. The covenant was sealed by the rite of circumcision, a rite which was to be performed on all the male children in Abraham's line.

Upon Abraham's death, his son Isaac became the leader of the people who had become known as the Hebrews, and the Lord renewed his covenant with Isaac and then with Jacob, Isaac's son. Jacob had twelve sons, who were to become founders of the twelve tribes of Israel. One of those sons, Joseph, was greatly envied by his brothers because he was Jacob's favorite. They plotted against Joseph and sold him into slavery in Egypt. But instead of leading a life of tragedy, Joseph became one of the most honored men in Egypt. He saved Egypt from a horrible famine and was able to bring Jacob and his eleven brothers and their families to Egypt, where they settled around the Nile valley about 1700 B.C.

The Hebrews lived in Egypt peacefully and prosperously until ca. 1580 B.C. when the friendly Hyksos dynasty fell, and the Theban pharaohs began to persecute them. The pharaohs considered the Hebrews a threat because they had grown so numerous, and one of the ways they persecuted the Jews was killing the male babies.

According to the Old Testament, the mother of Moses determined to save him and hid him in the rushes by a stream. The pharaoh's daughter found him and brought him up in the royal court. When Moses was a young man, the Lord came to him in the form of a burning bush and said: "I am the Lord. I appeared to Abraham, to Isaac, and to Jacob . . . and I have remembered my covenant. Say therefore to the people of Israel, 'I am the LORD, and I will bring you out from under the burdens

of the Egyptians . . . and I will take you for my people,
and I will be your God . . . who has brought you out
from under the burdens of the Egyptians. And I will
bring you into the land which I swore to give to Abraham, to Isaac, and to Jacob; I will give it to you for a
possession. I am the LORD' ".

Then the exodus began. Moses rescued Israel, helping his people to escape from the Egyptian soldiers by
parting the waters of the Red Sea for them. They wandered in the desert for forty days until they came to the
wilderness of Sinai.

The Lord then called to Moses and told him to go up
the mountain. There He made a new covenant with
Moses; He revealed to Moses the law that was to govern
the people of Israel forever after. It was a new and wider
covenant than the one the Lord had entered into with
Abraham. It was made with a people as a whole, and it
demanded great sacrifice on the part of the Israelites
and total dedication to their God. It consisted of 613
commandments; 365 of them referred to forbidden
things, and 248 to things that had to be done. The most
important were the first ten, referred to as the Ten
Commandments. The rest of the commandments concerned circumcision, diet, marriage, charity, neigh-
borly love, the Sabbath, and other festivals. The men of
the Levite tribe were to be the priests who would medi-
ate between God and the people. One family, that of
David, would forever after be the rulers of Israel. It was
a complete and detailed system of rules for living in
this world. It contained no mention of heaven and hell,
but out of it would gradually grow the idea of an ultimate resurrection of the dead at the "end of days."

On Sinai, the Lord also instructed Moses to have the

Israelites make an ark of wood, plated inside and out
with pure gold and carried on four wooden shafts and
to place inside it the two tablets on which the Ten
Commandments were written. This was the ark of the
covenant which the Israelites were thereafter to carry
with them as the symbol of their agreement with God.
The Lord also instructed them to construct a tent for a
tabernacle which would be the center for their worship
and the house for the ark. Thereafter, the people would
gather round it at the times of yearly festivals, the most
solemn being Passover, when deliverance from Egypt
was celebrated.

The Israelites continued on their way to Canaan,
entering the Holy Land about 1500 B.C. Moses saw
Canaan from Mount Nebo, but he was not destined to
enter Canaan with the people he had led there. He died
before they reached the Holy Land. Led by Joshua, the
Israelites conquered Canaan and settled down to what
they thought would be a peaceful history in the Promised Land.

But the history of the Jews in the Promised Land was
not to be peaceful. Struggles and jealousies broke out
among the leaders of the Israelites, and although an
attempt was made to bring about unity by the building
of a temple in Jerusalem to hold the ark, eventually the
nation was divided into two kingdoms. Once their nation had become divided, the Hebrew people lost their
sense of the Lord as the one God and saw him merely as
a national god, like the gods of other nations, and they
stopped living by the required standards. According to
the Scriptures, the angry Lord used the neighboring
nations of Assyria and Babylonia as tools to punish the
Hebrews. In 721 B.C. one of the neighboring kingdoms

was overcome by the Assyrians and its people forced into exile in Assyria. A century and a half later the other kingdom was overcome by the Babylonians who destroyed the temple in Jerusalem in 586 B.C. and held the people captive for some fifty years.

The Lord had not caused the destruction of the Hebrew kingdoms without first warning the Hebrew people. Indeed, whenever His people had begun to stray from the path that He had set before them, He had called certain men to preach the Word and to warn the people of their danger. It was these prophets who put together the Old Testament. Although the prophets were unable to prevent the Hebrews from bringing about their own destruction, in their writings they deepened the belief in one God that had arisen with Moses on Sinai. It was with the prophets that the concept of a Messiah first arose in Israel. The Messiah to whom they looked at this time was a king who would not be divine but who would be called the Son of God and who would unite Israel and lead it to the kingdom of God.

The Exile

The destruction of the temple marked a crucial turning point in the history of Israel, because the existence of the temple had ensured the continuity of Jewish traditions, traditions that had hardly changed since their beginning. Yet the prophet Jeremiah saw something positive in the tragedy, for he believed that the exile had shown the Israelites the universal meaning of God's will. God was not simply a national deity, and Judaism was not simply a national religion bound to one land until the moment when the Jewish people had left the Holy Land and been thrown into the hardships of captivity.

Separated from the Holy Land, the Jews dispersed, or scattered, elsewhere. Called the Diaspora, this dispersal proved to be a greater force for living by the Lord's laws than any that had existed before. The prophets concluded that the Jews themselves were responsible for their own misfortune because of their sinfulness, but at the same time they assured the people of God's forgiveness. The message was that the Jews had a personal relationship with God, one that did not depend upon Jerusalem, the temple, and sacrifices; one that meant that the Lord would be with them wherever they were. It was at this time that the prophets' vision of a kingdom of God in Israel became firmly associated with the uniting of Israel under a member of the house of David who would be "the Lord's anointed" and "the son of David."

But to earn such a kingdom the Jews would have to work very hard, and in the Diaspora the Jewish people observed a discipline unknown for years in the Holy Land. The center and driving force of Jewish life became the synagogue, which dates from that time. As the house of the Jews in exile, it filled the place of the temple. Prayers, rites, everything that took place in the synagogue pointed to the sorrow of the exile and often to the expectation of the Messiah.

Late in the seventh century B.C., the Babylonian exile ended and the center of Judaism was restored to Jerusalem. Although Jewish power was not restored in the Holy Land, the Persians, who took control in 536 B.C., and later the Greeks, did not persecute the Jews. In fact, under Persian rule the returned exiles were able to reunite and to feel a new sense of togetherness. The Torah, the original laws given by God to Moses, plus the writings of the prophets, became important to all the Jews again and helped to keep the people from turning to pagan gods.

But Judaism was still a young religion, and because of the Diaspora, different groups had developed different beliefs and practices. Religious disagreements often went hand in hand with political rivalries, and soon three great parties emerged: the Sadducees, the Pharisees, and the Essenes.

The Sadducees were priests and high officials. They stressed absolute obedience to the Torah and severely punished failure to obey. Because the Torah does not actually state that there is life after death, resurrection of the dead, and the eternity of soul, the Sadducees did not believe in them.

The Pharisees read the Torah with a free interpretation and accepted besides this written tradition the existence of an oral tradition, which gave the rabbis the authority to interpret the Torah and to adapt it to events in history. It was the Pharisees who defined what came to be the basic concepts of Judaism: the righteousness of God and the freedom of man; individual immortality; judgment after death; paradise, purgatory, and hell; resurrection of the dead; and the kingdom of God.

The Essenes were monastics who lived a life according to the Torah—a life of prayer, obedience, poverty, purity, and submission to God's will. They practiced the traditional rites—such as purification by water, communion with consecrated wine, the sharing of bread during meals resembling ritual sacrifices, communal prayers, study—in their full meaning. All these practices prepared the soul for the Last Judgment, the resurrection of the dead, and the kingdom of God. Teachers called scribes arose, dedicated to upholding the authority of the Torah and to adapting the biblical rules and laws to changes in conditions and circumstances.

The Romans overcame the Greeks and took Jerusalem in 63 B.C. Roman suppression of the Jews was merciless—Jews were crucified, deported, and sold as slaves by the thousands. In anguish the Jews prayed to God to send the Messiah to rescue them from their oppression and lead them into the kingdom of God.

At this time the faith of the Jews rested upon their expectation of the Messiah. Most traditions held that this Messiah would be a Messiah of Glory; but besides the tradition of the King of Glory, other traditions which appeared from the third century B.C., mention a mysterious Messiah, son of Joseph. According to these traditions, this Messiah would appear before the Messiah of Glory. His destiny was to be killed in Jerusalem while fighting for the redemption of Israel. Some believed also that the body of this Messiah would be hidden by angels and that he would appear again on the day of the triumph of the King of Glory.

Then, about A.D. 25, a man named Jesus of Nazareth began to achieve fame for his preaching and his miracles. Although he did not state that he was the Messiah, he was hailed by many as the Messiah. But this man preached humility and suffering and was not the Messiah of Glory expected by most Israelites. Although Jesus himself, the apostles, and the first members of the Christian Church were Jewish, Jews as a whole did not accept the crucified Christ as the fulfillment of messianic prophecy. And while the Christians proceeded to defeat the Roman idols, to upset the established order, and to carry the God of Israel to other nations, Israel chose a different path—one that was to mean great hardship.

In A.D. 66, the Jews began a war against Rome that was to go on until A.D. 135 when they would be crushed under terrible suppression and forced into exile in Galilee and Babylonia. The greatest catastrophe of the war occurred only four years after it began—in A.D. 70 the second temple in Jerusalem was destroyed. The event was considered the beginning of a new period of suffering and so important that the Jews began to date events from that time. Today the tragedy is mentioned daily in the liturgy of the synagogue, and its anniversary is observed every year by a day of fasting and mourning.

The temple had been the home of the God of Israel, the only place where it was possible to speak the name of the Lord, the only place where the sacrifices prescribed by the Torah could be performed. Separated once more from their land and with their temple again destroyed, the Jews were again in danger of losing contact with their God. But the rabbis were quick to see the disasters that had befallen Israel as part of the work of the Lord. The leaders of Israel saw the Romans as an instrument of God and the Roman victory, the destruction of the temple, and the exile as punishment for Israel's sins. But they did not believe that God had forsaken Israel. Instead, they saw their punishment as the beginning of payment for their sins. Thus, the whole people became like the suffering Messiah predicted by the rabbis, and through their suffering reached the state which Christ and, later, the scholars of Islam preached for all.

The task of the Jews was to preserve their heritage, no matter what hardships they endured and how much they were dispersed. With the destruction of the temple, the only sacred things were the Torah, the Oral Law, and the teachings of the scholars and rabbis who followed the tradition of Moses. Because the Torah was the only direct communication from God, it gained great prominence. Every one of its commandments that could still be followed (at least one-third of the commandments given on Sinai had become impossible to practice) was thought worthy of equal obedience, and the rabbis refused to see any difference between the small and great commandments. Where the Torah did not deal with a situation, the Oral Law and the teachings of the schools became the authorities. As the exile went on, the teaching of the scholars was put into writing. The resulting work, the Talmud ("teaching"), is definitely the most important work achieved by Judaism in exile.

The Talmud tries to give concrete knowledge of God's work and His will. It explains the relation between man and the land; man's duties in observing the solemnities and pilgrimages, fastings and festivals; the problems of marriage, sexual ethics, and vows; civil and penal law; holy matters having to do with the temple of Jerusalem; what things are pure and impure; and the laws governing the purification of men and women. The Talmud has remained almost unknown to non-Jews, while the Torah has become part of the heritage of the West. Yet, the Talmud is also important to the West, for it extends the written history of Judaism from a few centuries B.C., where the Torah ends, to the fifth century A.D. And particularly important, it contains the only witness of the birth of Christianity. St. Paul, perhaps the most famous Christian saint, was a Talmudist.

In addition to writing down their heritage, the Jewish people preserved it by turning away from the outside world, isolating themselves in their communities and in their faith.

The isolation of the Jewish communities became even greater when, with the conversion of the emperor Constantine, Christianity triumphed in the Roman Empire. The Jews, whose resistance to Christian influence angered the Christians, became known as the "God-killing people" and were forbidden to build or repair synagogues, excluded from all honorary posts, and forbidden to own Christian slaves (which meant that they were excluded from industry and large-scale agriculture). The worst blow came when the Romans abolished the patriarchate, the central authority of Judaism, in Jerusalem in A.D. 425, for now there was no central authority capable of ruling on religious matters for all of Israel. According to the traditional law, only the Messiah could reestablish the central authority, and thus the hope for the Messiah increased in intensity.

Then, in the middle of the seventh century, Judaism was revitalized both spiritually and economically by the rise of Islam. Islam arose as a religion powerfully inspired by Judaism. In fact, the followers of Islam worshiped the God of Abraham and claimed to be the spiritual descendants of Abraham. So close were the two religions that many Jews were converted to Islam, and Islam's greatest early successes were in cities that had powerful Jewish communities. The spread of the Islamic empire, from India to the Atlantic Ocean and from Arabia to the Pyrenees, also helped to spread the Talmud and other writings to the communities of the Diaspora.

Economically, the change brought on by the rise and expansion of Islam was even greater. Islam was generally tolerant of the Jews, and for the first time since the exile began, Jews were free to engage in industry and commerce. Jews by the thousands left their small farms and manual jobs to seek jobs in the large Islamic cities as tradesmen and craftsmen. Soon, a wealthy Jewish middle class arose.

The one major disadvantage to Judaism of the rise and growth of Islam was that the unity and tradition of Israel were endangered. At the end of the seventh century, the rise of Islam brought about the rise of the strongest nonreligious movement that Israel had known. The communities of the Diaspora had been united chiefly by the belief, disseminated by the rabbis, that the suffering of the Israelites was necessary to Israel's redemption. With greater freedom and acceptance under the reign of Islam, some Jews began to question the necessity of continuing to follow the law of the Talmud.

While Islam flourished, the problems of Israel were mainly internal problems of faith. But when, in the tenth century, the Islamic empire began to break up, many external problems beset the Jews. The Arabs began to treat the Jews as second-class citizens, although they never persecuted the Jews as the Christians had.

When the Christian Crusaders had conquered the Holy Land, the Jews were forced to emigrate from it—

either because they were unwilling to live under the oppression of the Christians or because they were expelled. The Jews migrated west, to Spain, where a sizable Jewish community already existed, and to England, France, and Germany where some Jews had already settled to engage in commerce and industry. But these countries were Christian, and soon the Jews in these countries were being attacked as the people who had murdered Christ, and subjected to many degradations. They were made to wear round or pointed hats that distinguished them from other Europeans, forced to live in special districts known from the sixteenth century on as ghettos, and denied all occupations except trade, craftsmanship, and money-lending. Eventually, Jews were banished from England in 1290, from France in 1394, and from Spain in 1492. But in those countries that did not banish them, the Jews found a kind of protection in their ghettos, and as they had done before in their history, they withdrew into their ghettos and devoted themselves to prayer and the study of biblical and talmudic literature. It was then that Jewish mysticism gained its greatest influence.

Strains of mysticism had appeared before in Jewish history. The mystical tradition is known as the Cabala, which means "knowledge that is received." Since its beginning it has complemented the Bible and the Talmud without contradicting them. But in mysticism, a much greater emphasis was placed upon the fate of the soul which, depending upon the kind of life one had lived, could be either eternal bliss or eternal punishment. From the beginning, the Cabala stressed the doctrine of the transmigration of souls—the belief that at death the soul passes from one body into another—a doctrine that is completely foreign to the talmudic tradition.

In the fifteenth and sixteenth centuries, the intensity of the Cabala was increased tenfold. In 1492, the Spanish Inquisition reached its height, and the Jews in Spain were subjected to one of the cruelest trials in Jewish history. Not only were they tortured and murdered by the thousands, but, because they were expelled from the country, their main center of cabalistic studies was destroyed. In reaction to this anti-Semitism, the Jews devoted all their energies to bring about the end of the exile. Through intense prayer and self-sacrifice, the Jews would force open the doors of the redemption. So intense was the yearning for release that Jews all over Europe turned to the Cabala, and in fact the cabalist movement was the last great spiritual movement to sweep through Judaism.

The end of the exile could be brought about only by a return to the Holy Land and the reinstitution of the central authority that had been destroyed by the Romans. But according to Jewish law, only the Messiah could restore the continuity of the sacraments and reinstate the priesthood in Israel. Many attempts were made to resolve this problem, but to no avail, and the resulting frustration and impatience of the Jews prepared them to believe that the Messiah of Glory was close at hand.

The last original religious expression of Judaism in exile arose in the eighteenth century—Hasidism. The founder of the movement, a Ukranian rabbi named Israel ben Eliezer, better known as Baal Shem Tov, wished to create an awareness of the presence of God in every creature and of the total dedication of man to God and to his fellow men. It was a quiet mysticism, not excited and zealous like many earlier mystical movements, and it gained great popularity in all the Jewish communities of Eastern Europe. The Hasidim formed their own communities and continued to popularize the basic themes of the Cabala while at the same time reinterpreting them in order to make them more available to the masses.

When Baal Shem Tov died in 1760, an estimated half the Jews in Europe were his followers. After his death, the movement split into many sections and weakened.

The Modern Era

The discovery of the New World, the economic and political revolutions in Europe, and the split within the Christian Church brought about by the Protestant Reformation all combined to make the world outside the ghettos much more open to the Jews. In 1791, France became the first nation in Europe to grant equal rights to Jews, and France's lead was followed by Germany in 1848, England in 1858, Austria-Hungary in 1867, Italy in 1870, and Russia in 1917.

Now that they had been granted equal rights, the Jews felt less need of the practices and traditions that for almost two thousand years had kept them together and given them a reason for being while they were persecuted and treated as second-class citizens. Confronted with Christian society and lacking the protective walls of the ghetto, the Jews were made aware of important alternatives to their convictions and beliefs. Most obvious were the changes in dress, language, jobs, and even names that took place within the Jewish community as the Jews attempted to fit into the larger society. It was argued that Judaism had to be adapted to the needs of the modern world—a new set of standards was required.

The Jewish reform movement began in Germany, also the birthplace of the Protestant Reformation. After 1840, it spread from Germany to England and France and finally to America, which proved to be the ideal place for it to grow.

From the beginning of the reform movement, the traditionalists within the Jewish community had attacked the new tendencies. In the face of the new liberalism they had remained even more faithful to the traditional and sacred world of the Torah, Talmud, and Cabala. They had decided not to accept anything from the outside world that would not completely fit in with their divine duty. They were determined to suffer humiliation and death for the love of the Messiah of Glory and to remain in the ghettos until he called them to return. In the face of the threat of the reform movement, the traditionalists resisted in every way, denouncing reformers to the Jewish authorities, refusing to bury their dead, etc. Resistance was so strong in the Jewish communities in Poland, Russia, the Near East, and Prussia that Reform Judaism never gained a foothold there.

The conflict between reform and counter-reform movements threatened to destroy Judaism altogether, for many Jews, faced with a choice between a conservative religion that rejected the changing times and a liberal religion that was empty of faith and discipline, chose neither and simply assimilated themselves into the dominant culture.

But as had happened before in the history of the Hebrews, once again spiritual disintegration caused by problems within the Jewish community was checked by much greater problems—in this case by the near annihilation of the Jews in Germany and eastern Europe. Between 1940 and 1945 the great European centers of Jewish life were violently and almost completely exterminated by the German Nazis.

Then on May 14, 1948, the British army that had occupied Palestine since the end of World War I (officially, since 1923) returned control of the area to the Jews, and after nearly two thousand years of exile the people of Israel were again united with their land. Soon, Jews from all over the world were arriving in Palestine, having left their homes and neighbors and jobs to begin an exciting but difficult new life in a brand-new state. Each group of Jews brought with it particular beliefs and practices, and the gathering in Israel of Jews from seventy-four different countries revealed just how varied Judaism had become over the long years of the Diaspora. There were Yemenite Jews who had changed little since the beginning of the exile and who reflected the spirit of those who had first begun to write down the Oral Law. There were African Jews whose religion had changed little since the pre-Islamic period of Jewish history, and their neighbors, the North African Jews, who brought the gentleness inherited from the golden age of Moslem Spain. There were Cabalists and Talmudists, and Hasidim who still dressed in long black coats and wore side curls and long beards. There were also Jews from America who had grown up in the reform tradition and Jews from the Near East and Eastern Europe who had hardly been touched by the reform.

One group of Jews who were not represented were the Lubavitchers, a Hasidic group who claim to be the descendants of the original Baal Shem Tov and their descent through seven rebbes, or leaders. Their ideal is to live exactly according to the Torah, following its 613 laws and prescriptions even in the midst of the modern world. Because they believe that only the Messiah can re-establish Israel, they do not support the state of Israel.

After World War II, many of the few surviving Jews of Eastern Europe were able to immigrate to the United States. Rabbi Menachem M. Schneerson, the seventh Lubavitcher Rebbe, and his followers settled in Brooklyn, New York, where they established a community that has become vital and influential.

The Lubavitcher Hasidim enjoy what Israel does not—a strong, centralized religious authority. In their attempts to include all the Jews of the Diaspora who wanted to be part of Israel, the founders of the new state created a complicated political system. Under this system of proportional representation, each group or sect can form its own political party. Candidates are chosen by the party, voters cast their ballots for a party, and seats in the Israeli Knesset, or parliament, are allotted to each party according to its share of the vote. As long as the parties which together controlled the majority of the seats were in general agreement politically, they were able to form coalition governments and make major decisions.

But this system began to break down with the rise of Jewish fundamentalism in the last quarter of the twentieth century. Corresponding in time to the growth of fundamentalism in the two other major Western religions—Christianity and Islam—ultra-Orthodox rabbis

who disdain Israeli statehood and right-wing ex-
tremists who want to expel all non-Jews from Israel and
Israeli-occupied territories have led a resurgence of
fundamentalism.

Since the middle 1980s, small fundamentalist political parties have increased their representation in the
Knesset so that the government has been evenly split
and thus all but paralyzed in its ability to make decisions. In the late 1980s, right-wing Israelis began to
establish new settlements in the Israeli-occupied territories of the West Bank and Gaza Strip, sparking an
intifada, or revolt, on the part of the Palestinian Arabs
living in those areas. Other groups have moved into the
Christian quarter of Jerusalem, calling into question the
future of Christianity in one of its holiest cities.

Thus, although the Israelites and their land have
been reunited and the physical Diaspora has ended,
with the exception of groups like the Lubavitchers, a
spiritual Diaspora still exists. Judaism today is marked
not only by a variety of beliefs and practices but also by
widely varied political ideas. A problem faces Israel
that the Jews, by the very nature of their strongest
beliefs, cannot solve themselves. No central authority
capable of ruling on religious matters for the whole
community exists or has existed since the destruction
of the temple and the abolition of the patriarchate by
the Romans. Only the Messiah can establish this central authority.

Judaism continues to wait for the Messiah. The real
tragedy and at the same time the greatness of the religion is that Jews have never doubted the coming of the
King of Glory but have remained faithful in their suffering.

Jewish Religious Practices

The most universal of Jewish rituals is *kashruth*, the dietary laws, for these are observed by the faithful in the very act of eating to sustain life. In the revelation to Moses on Sinai, God distinguished between foods, prohibiting the eating of those that were unclean, and also forbade the Jews to boil a young animal in its mother's milk, or to eat an animal's blood. These biblical prohibitions are retained in the well-known dietary regulations still observed by Orthodox Jews, although contemporary Reform Judaism has rejected these laws. Orthodox Jews do not eat pork, shellfish, or other scavenger animals; they do not eat meat and milk at the same meal; and they eat only animals slaughtered in a prescribed manner that involves disposing of much of the blood. The term *kosher* refers to food that may be eaten. Some of these laws, such as the one prohibiting the eating of scavengers, are obviously based on sound hygienic or economic reasoning; others are still the subject of scholarly discussion.

Almost as important as the dietary laws is the system governing prayer. Orthodox Jews divide their day into three periods of prayer: in the morning, the prayer of Shaharit, which for some is preceded and followed by an hour of meditation; at noon, the prayer of Minha, the offering, which recalls the daily sacrifice offered in the temple at Jerusalem before the exile; and at dusk, the prayer of Arbit, which ushers in the peace of the night. The daily prayers prepare for the Sabbath, which marks the accomplishment of creation.

Three Jewish festivals, established by the Bible, mark the times when God intervened in Israel's history. Passover (March or April) marks the coming out of Egypt and deliverance from captivity. Since the Jews led by Moses left Egypt very quickly, they did not have time to allow their dough to rise. So they baked flat, unleavened cakes (matzoth), which are to this day eaten during Passover. Shabuoth is the Feast of Weeks, celebrated on the fiftieth day after Passover; it commemorates the revelation at Mt. Sinai. Sukkoth, a harvest festival, commemorates the temporary shelter Israel found in the desert.

Other holy days and festivals include Rosh Hashanah, which celebrates the creation of the world, and Yom Kippur (Day of Atonement), a day of fasting and prayer, when the ultimate judgment and mercy of the Lord are awaited.

Thus, there are daily, weekly, and yearly rhythms of prayer, and they show the basic requirements of Judaism: through prayer, enlightened by study, man attains knowledge of God and salvation. Man must prove his submission by obeying the commandments of the Torah, commandments which ensure a divine and earthly communion that safeguards his spiritual life and unity.

IV

Christianity

IN A WAY, CHRISTIANITY IS A FURTHER STAGE OF JUDA-
ism. Many events that occurred or were predicted in
Judaism were either paralleled or fulfilled in Christianity. The Old Testament of the Christian Bible is
entirely Jewish history. The history of Judaism is the
story of Israel and God's attempt to prepare a particular
community of people to make His ways known to the
rest of the world. What separates Christians from Jews
is belief in Jesus Christ as the Son of God, and the story
of Christianity is really the story of Jesus Christ and of
the worship of Christ as Savior. In Christianity, the
"chosen people" of God are all those who believe in
God and in Jesus Christ, the Son whom God sent to be
their savior.

The Life of Christ

Jesus was born in the town of Nazareth in the region
of Galilee, in the northern part of present-day Israel. At
the time of Jesus's birth, the whole area was part of the
Roman empire, and the era was probably in the middle
of the eighth century of Rome. According to the New
Testament, Jesus, like Buddha, was born of a virgin. His
young mother, Mary, was betrothed to Joseph, who was
of the house of David. But before the two were married
the young Mary was visited by the Angel Gabriel, who
said to her: "Hail, O favored one, the Lord is with
you! . . . Do not be afraid, Mary, for you have found
favor with God. And behold, you wil conceive in your
womb and bear a son, and you shall call his name
Jesus. He will be great, and will be called the Son of the
Most High; and the Lord God will give him the throne
of his father David, and he will reign over the house of
Jacob for ever; and of his kingdom there will be no
end. . . . The Holy Spirit will come upon you, and the
power of the Most High will overshadow you; therefore
the child to be born will be called holy, the Son of
God".

Just before Jesus was born, Caesar Augustus, the Roman emperor, issued a decree for a census of the population of the empire, and Joseph took Mary, his
betrothed, who was by now heavy with child, to his
native town of Bethlehem in order to register. They
could find no suitable lodging place in Bethlehem and
had to stay in a stable behind an inn. There Mary gave
birth to Jesus.

On the night Jesus was born, many signs appeared to
herald his birth. The Star of David rose over Bethlehem,

and an angel appeared to three shepherds in the countryside close by to announce the birth of a savior, Christ the Lord. In Jerusalem, three wise men appeared before King Herod and asked him where they could find the king of the Jews; they had seen his star as it rose and had come to pay homage. Herod was disturbed by this news, and made plans to kill this child who was to be king of the Jews. But an angel appeared to Joseph in a dream and warned him to escape into Egypt with Mary and the child. Joseph did so, and the family remained in Egypt until Herod was dead. Then they went back to Galilee, to the town of Nazareth.

Joseph was a carpenter, and although he seems to have been the only carpenter in Nazareth, he was probably often hard pressed to support his large family. In addition to Jesus, the oldest son, Joseph and his wife Mary had four other sons, James, Joseph, Jude, and Simon, and at least two daughters. Like other young Jewish boys, Jesus very early learned by heart certain verses of the Law, and by the time he was ten or twelve, he had become a "Son of the Commandment" and had to obey the Law. He also learned that his people were in the "last days" and that soon the Messiah would reign on earth.

When he was twelve, Jesus was allowed to accompany his parents on their yearly journey to Jerusalem for the Feast of the Passover. Jerusalem must have been farther away from home than Jesus had ever been, for the journey took four days. And the city was unlike anything he had seen before, with its huge towers, thousands of people, and bustling activity. But he was probably not so awed that he did not notice the Roman soldiers blocking the entrance to the city or hear the insulting remarks of the Sadducees and the loud preaching of the Pharisees. He must have gotten an inkling of the hatred and rivalry and the oppression of the foreigners who dominated Israel's land.

When the festival was over, Joseph and Mary set off with the Nazareth caravan to return home and had gone a day's journey before they discovered that Jesus was not with them. Returning to Jerusalem to look for him, they found him in the temple listening to and questioning the scholars. His parents had been greatly worried over his absence, but when they asked their son why he had caused them so much worry, he answered: "How is it that you sought me? Did you not know that I must be in my Father's house?" They did not understand what he was saying; perhaps Jesus did not really understand what he was saying either.

Soon after the return from Nazareth Jesus began to learn his father's trade; it was customary for the oldest son to do so in order to help support the family. And when, after a time, his father died, Jesus became the family provider.

For long years, Jesus worked at his trade and supported his family. But at the same time he seems to have devoted himself to "his Father's affairs." He became a rabbi, a position that required much more knowledge than was ordinarily taught in the regular schools. Thus, while he was working as a carpenter, Jesus must have devoted considerable time to study. After he had become a rabbi, Jesus, like other rabbis, healed the sick, counseled the unhappy and weary, and had disciples to whom he taught the things he had learned.

When Jesus was almost thirty years old, he heard about a young man called John the Baptist who claimed to have been called by God to go out among the people of Israel and tell them that the kingdom of heaven was near. The Baptist urged the people to repent their sins and baptized those who did repent and wanted to be saved. He had built up quite a following, and crowds came to him wherever he preached. Intrigued by the stories of passing travelers and anxious to hear this Baptist for himself, Jesus set out to find him. He found the Baptist on the banks of the Jordan, preaching in an urgent voice that had a strong influence upon the crowd gathered to listen to him. Jesus was profoundly impressed by this man, who seemed to have no ambitions for power and fame, whose only concern was to warn Israel that time was short. He stepped forward and asked to be baptized.

When John heard Jesus' request, he said, "I need to be baptized by you, and do you come to me?" But Jesus answered, "Let it be so now; for thus it is fitting for us to fulfill all righteousness." John gave in and baptized Jesus, submerging him in the waters of the Jordan, and when Jesus came up from the water the heavens suddenly opened, and the Spirit of God descended like a dove and landed upon him. And a voice from heaven said, "This is my beloved Son, with whom I am well pleased".

Jesus now had proof that he had a divine calling—a calling which the story of the temple shows he had somehow felt even as a child. The voice had told him that he was the Son of God, the Messiah, but he was unsure exactly what sort of Messiah he should be.

Jesus went out into the wilderness to be alone and to think. He spent forty days and forty nights there. During this time he was often tempted by the devil, who urged him to perform feats of glory to dazzle the world if he was really the Messiah. Jesus knew that the Messiah was supposed to be a great king who would dominate and awe and lead Israel to glory, and he was tempted to become that kingly Messiah. But gradually Jesus realized that God had not chosen him to work any magical transformations. The kingdom of God should be invisible, present wherever repentance and a new birth of the soul occurred. The Messiah should work to change the hearts of the Jews and after that worldly reforms would be a natural result.

When he came out of the wilderness, Jesus learned that John the Baptist had been arrested, and he decided to take up the work that John had been doing. He preached repentance and baptized people who wanted to be saved. At first he preached in the area of Nazareth, but people who had known him since he was a child found it hard to take him seriously, and he decided to leave. His family could not understand him and criticized him for not settling down.

After a painful farewell to his family, Jesus went to Capernaum, on the borders of Zebulun and Naphtali. Soon after he arrived, he was walking by the Sea of Galilee when he came upon two men fishing. Without even talking with them he somehow knew that he needed them. He told them to follow him and become fishers of men, and Simon, whom Jesus renamed Peter (from a Greek root meaning "rock"), and Andrew became his first two disciples. On the same day, John and James left their boat and their father and followed him also. Eventually, Jesus would gather around him twelve disciples whom he hoped would restore the twelve tribes of Israel and thus a kingdom of God on earth.

In Capernaum, Jesus and his disciples rented a house, but he did most of his preaching outside, on the shore of a lake. He proclaimed pardon and mercy at a time when the people of Israel heard only about laws of blood and vengeance, gods of jealousy and gloom. He told the people to love their enemies and to forgive, for the meek would inherit the earth. If they resorted to violence or even had violent thoughts, they would not only be playing into the hands of their enemies but also abandoning the path that God had marked out for them as a kingdom of priests and a holy nation to win the heathen to God. They would be behaving like the rest of the nations and would be unworthy of the kingdom of God.

Jesus also spent a great deal of time healing the sick, and it was word of his healing that drew the largest number of people to hear and see him. The crowds were astonished to see the lame walking, the blind with their sight restored, the deaf able to hear, and they whispered that this Jesus of Nazareth must be the Messiah. Some even asked him if he was the Messiah, but Jesus would not proclaim himself the Messiah until the hearts of the people had changed or at least had begun to change. He insisted that all his healing was accomplished by prayer.

Jesus preached in Galilee without encountering opposition from the authorities, but eventually the Pharisees became jealous of his popularity and afraid of his influence over the people. They began to spy upon him, investigate his background, publicly question his faith. They criticized him for not washing his hands when he ate and for eating types of food that were forbidden by the dietary laws. Jesus answered that it was not neglecting to wash one's hands or eating forbidden food that made a man unclean, but what he said and how he acted. He was tired of hearing about things pure and impure when he knew how impure the Pharisees' and indeed the Jews' minds were. As Jesus ignored the laws of Judaism more and more, the Pharisees' attacks upon him became more violent, and his answering words became more scathing.

The spying and other types of harassment by the Pharisees became so unbearable for Jesus that he left Capernaum and began a wandering ministry. Everywhere he went he was recognized, and he drew great crowds. One time, by the shore of a lake, the crowds cried that he was the Messiah and demanded that he proclaim himself. When he would not, the crowd became angry. After that, Jesus began to visit the Gentiles (non-Jews), whom the Jews considered uncivilized. Jewish law forbade Jews to enter the houses of Gentiles, and it was thought that Jews who did so would become unclean. But Jesus had found that many non-Jews listened to and accepted his preaching better than many Jews. He began to say that non-Jews would reach the kingdom of heaven before many Jews did.

But the Jews, no matter how far they had strayed from the path set for them by God, were still the descendants of Abraham and of Moses, the people whom God had chosen, and Jesus' mission was to save Israel. The prophets had foreseen that the Messiah of suffering would die a violent death, and Jesus began to realize that perhaps it would indeed take his own death to save Israel. Perhaps only that could accomplish what he could not accomplish in life—a change in men's hearts.

The prophets had foretold that the Messiah of suffer-

ing would die in Jerusalem. But before going there,
Jesus returned to Capernaum, where his mother and
brothers had moved. When they urged him to perform
some act that would prove he was the Messiah, Jesus
realized that they still did not understand. Sad but
determined, he set out for Jerusalem.

On the way, Jesus called his disciples together and
told them, "Behold, we are going up to Jerusalem; and
the Son of man will be delivered to the chief priests and
scribes, and they will condemn him to death, and deliver him to the Gentiles to be mocked and scourged
and crucified, and he will be raised on the third day."
He then instructed his disciples to go before him and
prepare for his entry into Jerusalem by obtaining an ass
and a colt of an ass in order to fulfill the prophecy:

> Tell the daughter of Zion,
> Behold, your king is coming to you,
> humble, and mounted on an ass,
> and on a colt, the foal of an ass.

Accordingly, Jesus entered the city on the back of an ass
and a colt of an ass, and the crowds spread palm
branches in his path and hailed him as the son of
David.

Once in Jerusalem, Jesus immediately went to the
temple, which was really little more than a market
because of all the people buying and selling goods
there. He overturned the merchants' tables, accusing
them of turning the temple into a robbers' den. He also
argued with the Pharisees, who tried to trick him into
saying something against the Roman authorities—
something for which he could be arrested. When Jesus
cleverly answered them without saying anything in-

criminating, they resolved to arrest him anyway, but
secretly, so that the people would not witness it. Then
the disciple Judas Iscariot went to the priests and offered to betray Jesus for money; the priests gave him
thirty silver pieces, and from then on Judas looked for
an opportunity to betray Jesus.

A few days later, Jesus and his disciples met for the
Passover meal, and he told them that one of them
would betray him. He then broke bread and gave it to
them, saying that it was his body, and he passed around
a cup of wine, saying that it was his blood. After they
had sung psalms, they went to the Mount of Olives and
to the garden of the small estate of Gethsemane. The
disciples settled down for the night, and Jesus went off
to pray, for he knew what was in store for him. At one
point he fell to the ground and prayed, "My Father, if it
be possible, let this cup pass from me; nevertheless, not
as I will, but as thou wilt".

After a while, Jesus returned to find the disciples
asleep, and he awakened them to tell them that the
hour of his betrayal was near. He was still speaking
when Judas appeared, followed by a band of Roman
soldiers. Judas approached Jesus and kissed him, and
at this prearranged signal the Roman soldiers stepped
forward and arrested Jesus. Jesus had also told his
disciples that they would deny him, and as he had
foretold, they ran away.

The Roman soldiers took Jesus to the Roman court
and brought him before Pontius Pilate, the governor of
the city. Then he was questioned and mocked. The
guards stripped him and made him wear a red cloak
and a crown of thorns and placed a reed in his hand,
and then they laughingly knelt down to him and hailed

him as king of the Jews. Witnesses came forward to testify to things he had said. The Jewish priests charged that he had tried to incite the Jewish people to riot and urged Pilate to order his crucifixion. Pilate refused, saying he had found no case against Jesus, but the crowd whom the priests had called to the courts shouted "Crucify him!" over and over. Finally, Pilate gave in to the people and handed Jesus over to be crucified.

Immediately, he was taken to the hill of Calvary, where he was nailed to a cross between two thieves who were also being crucified. On the cross, Jesus cried, "Father, forgive them; for they know not what they do". The soldiers mocked him, and divided his clothes among themselves. The Pharisees also mocked him, saying that if he was the Christ, he should save himself.

When Jesus had been on the cross for six hours, he cried, "Father, into thy hands I commit my spirit" and died. And darkness covered the land for three hours, and all those who had mocked and jeered realized what they had done.

Jesus' followers took his body, wrapped it in a shroud, and laid it in a stone tomb. On the third day, the women who had come from Galilee with Jesus went to the tomb with spices and ointments, but when they reached the tomb, they found the stone rolled away and the body of Jesus gone.

That evening Jesus appeared to the eleven apostles as they sat at their meal. In their awe they were unable to speak, and Jesus said, "These are my words which I spoke to you, while I was still with you, that everything written about me in the law of Moses and the prophets and the psalms must be fulfilled. . . . Thus it is written, that the Christ should suffer and on the third day rise from the dead, and that repentance and forgiveness of sins should be preached in his name to all nations, beginning from Jerusalem. You are witnesses of these things". Thus, just as it was written in the Scriptures, Jesus gave his own life for the sins of the Jews and for those other nations who would come to believe in God.

The Early Christians

The eleven disciples knew that they had seen a miracle, and, with such inspiration, were eager to spread the word about Christ and his message. Soon they separated and went out to different centers of the Roman Empire, reciting the events of Jesus' life, and urging the people to prepare for his coming again, which they hoped would happen very soon. Many people heard and believed what the apostles said, and communities of Christians arose wherever the message reached. As people chosen by God shortly before the world was to end, they set themselves consciously apart from the worldy life around them, forming communities based on ties of love and mutual concern and living lives based on the life of Jesus.

These communities were not isolated from one another without any central authority, for before his death, Jesus had laid the foundation of the Christian Church. One day he had asked his disciples who they thought he was. Peter had immediately answered that he was the Christ, the Son of Man, and Jesus had replied, "Blessed are you, Simon Bar-Jona! For flesh and blood has not revealed this to you, but my Father who is in heaven. And I tell you, you are Peter, and on this rock I will build my church. . . . I will give you the keys of the kingdom of heaven, and whatever you loose on earth shall be loosed in heaven" Thus, Peter was the highest authority of Christianity, followed closely by the other apostles, and the oral collections of Jesus' sayings comprised the law of the Christian community.

Although some of the early Christians were Jews, in general the Christian message that Jesus had been the Christ, and the fulfillment of the promises originally made by God to Abraham, Isaac, and Jacob, encountered great opposition within Judaism, and soon the apostles turned to the gentile world.

The gentile world was basically the world of the Roman Empire which, in the first century A.D., was great and powerful and rich. The masses worshiped popular gods, although other cults were strong. One such cult was that of emperor worship, in which emperors were seen as responsible for peace and were worshiped for maintaining it. Also, mystery religions abounded; characterized by superstition and secrecy, they were based on worship by an individual of one particular god who in return gave the worshiper mystical powers. But although these cults offered thrilling and mystical individual experiences, they gave the worshipers no sense of community.

The Christian apostles realized that their success in converting the Gentiles would depend greatly upon the needs that the Christian doctrine could fill. And thus, in the gentile world they did not stress the coming of Christ as the fulfillment of Jewish prophecy but rather as the beginning of a new era. Christ was lord over a new people, created by him and on whom God had poured his spirit, an Israel of God in which could be found the forgiveness of sin.

This gospel, or "good news," was eagerly received by the Gentiles, and the Christian movement grew quickly. But denouncing pagan practices such as the worship of Caesar brought upon the early Christians the suspicion of fellow citizens and even persecution by the Roman authorities. Nevertheless, Christian churches continued to arise in many parts of the Roman Empire, attracting Romans of every social class.

The spread of the Church further into the Greco-Roman world was one of the reasons for the writing of the Gospels (the first four books of the New Testament), for the Christian message was coming into contact with many different types of people and their religions. The need was felt to emphasize the life of Jesus, to root the idea of Christianity in the life of a real man. Word-of-mouth teachings could not reach as many people as written documents could. Also, the persecutions by the Roman authorities caused some to believe that Christianity was in danger of being suppressed, and a written tradition could be preserved more easily than an oral one. Another reason the Gospels were written was the growing realization on the part of the Christians that the end of earthly life was not as near as they had thought. While they believed it was close at hand, there was no need to put the story of Jesus in writing, but the delay of the end made a written account possible. The eyewitness to the life of Jesus were passing away, and their testimony had to be preserved.

Church tradition holds that the first Gospel was written by Matthew, and accordingly his version comes first in the New Testament. But the Gospels of Matthew, Mark, and Luke are all concerned with the life of Christ, from his birth to his crucifixion. They differ in the chronology of the events of Jesus' life and in emphasis, depending upon what new people they were written for. The other books of the New Testament are not concerned with the actual events of Jesus' life but attempt to relate teachings to the lives of the Christians and to explain the relations of the Christians with the government, with other religions, and with each other. It is generally accepted that all the books of the New Testament were written within one hundred years of Jesus's death, which is placed around A.D. 30. Thus, the New Testament contrasts sharply with the Old Testament, which spans at least ten centuries.

The Gospels were not the earliest New Testament documents, although they are usually placed first. The earliest documents of Christianity are the Epistles (letters) of Paul.

Paul was probably a Roman citizen, born a Jew and proud of it. Throughout his life he proclaimed himself "a Pharisee, son of a Pharisee." In fact, before he was converted to Christianity, he was a bitter persecutor of the early Christians. But one day, about A.D. 34, on the road to Damascus he had a vision of the risen Jesus that changed his life. From then on, Paul dedicated his life to serving Christ, who had personally chosen him as his follower. He was destined to become the greatest missionary to the pagans, but he believed that salvation was for the Jews, and he offered the gospel that he preached to them first. Although he had little success in the synagogues, his concern with his own people persisted. His vision of Jesus had been as the Messiah, and he kept the Jewish law all his life.

Paul was far more industrious and far more often in prison for the sake of the gospel than any other Christian. He traveled far and wide—to Jerusalem, Syria, Cilicia, Cyprus, Lycaonia, and many other parts of the Roman Empire, and it is possible that he even traveled to Spain. Thirteen documents—about one-quarter of the New Testament—are attributed to him, and according to a very ancient tradition, he was martyred in Rome in A.D. 67. His thirteen letters to converted Gentiles in various areas stress the meaning of Jesus and his importance for the life of the Church, and they have continued to influence the later history of Christianity. Indeed, some have argued that many of the most creative movements in the history of Church have been born of a rediscovery of Paul, including the Protestant Reformation.

For nearly two centuries after the death of Christ, the Christian movement spread, sometimes tolerated by the Roman emperors, sometimes persecuted, but always growing. Then, in the beginning of the fourth century, Emperor Constantine the Great converted to Christianity and eventually proclaimed it the official religion of the empire. After that, except for a brief revival of paganism under Julian (who died in 363), Christianity in some form was the religion of the Roman emperors, as it was of the Germanic tribes who eventually conquered the empire. Europe had become Christian, along with great sections of the Middle East and North Africa, although after Muslims swept through the world on their missions of conversion, it was largely supplanted in the Middle East and North Africa by Islam.

Under the Roman emperors, the first general councils were held to solve the controversies within Christianity. Disagreement had long existed over various doctrines, and two of the most important doctrinal disputes were decided in the councils of the fourth, fifth, and sixth centuries. One concerned the relationship between God, Jesus, and the Holy Spirit. Some Christian sects felt that God comprised all three. Others felt that God could not be the Father and the Son and the Holy Spirit at the same time. The former sects prevailed at the councils, and the idea of God in three "persons," Father (creative aspect), Son (earthly aspect), and Holy Spirit (supernatural aspect) became official Christian doctrine. This decision opened the way for the solution of another controversy. Many sects did not consider Christ equal to God, but the decision that both Christ and God were comprised within God made it follow naturally that Christ, the eternal Son of God, was equal with God the Father.

As Christianity became firmly established in the Roman Empire, Constantinople, the eastern capital, came to rival Rome as the central authority of Christianity. With the Great Schism of 1054, Christianity became divided into eastern and western sects. The separation between the eastern and western parts of the Church has been a fact for about half of Christian history.

Eastern (Byzantine) Christianity became known as Orthodox, and it spread into other parts of Eastern Europe, where it took hold as a series of national churches which owed only a formal allegiance to the Patriarch of Constantinople (in present-day Turkey). It was introduced into Russia by Greek missionaries from Byzantium and became the religion of the state of Kiev, now the provincial capital of the Ukraine, in 988. Spreading throughout Russia and its border states, the Orthodox Church spawned local variants. For example, the Ukrianian Church for many years belonged to a group of churches in Eastern Europe and the Middle East which followed the rites of the Eastern Orthodox Church but maintained loyalty to the pope in Rome. But in Russia, the Eastern Orthodox Church as a whole departed so much from Byzantine Orthodoxy that in 1439 it declared itself independent as the Russian Orthodox Church. Today, the Russian Orthodox Church is the largest Eastern Orthodox church in the world.

One major difference between the Russian and Eastern Orthodox churches is the greater secularism of Russian Orthodoxy, and its willingness to respond to government authority. This comparative secularism helped it to survive under Communism, which will be discussed in the next section. Nor has it ever been as centralized as the Roman Church.

Roman Christianity became highly centralized because of the power and prestige of the popes, successors of Peter, whose absolute authority the Eastern Orthodox Church denies. From the time of the division between the Eastern and Western churches, it also moved farther away from the original teachings of Christ. This was due partly to the need of the masses for a religion that they could understand—idols to worship; ceremonies, priests, and other mediators between God and the worshiper; more earthly and worldly elements. Original Christianity, just like the original forms of other religions, changed as it came into contact with more and more people. And like other religions, although it became stronger for a while, eventually the ceremonies and rituals and priests became more important than the original teachings of Jesus. The God of love and mercy Jesus had spoken of gave way to a harsh, judging God. It was this God whom militant European Christians called upon to help them in the Crusades against "heathens and infidels" in the eleventh century. A series of military expeditions that extended over two centuries, the Crusades were aimed at Muslim powers that had gained a foothold in the traditional holy lands of Christianity. This same era was also one of intense Christian persecution of Jews in Europe.

In the later Middle Ages, various protest movements arose that rejected the strong authority, rigidity, and ritualism that they said the Church had sunk into. The leaders of most of these movements did not wish to overthrow the authority of the papacy but merely wanted to bring about a reformation of the doctrine and life of the Church from within.

Martin Luther did not set out to bring about a radical transformation of the Church. He simply believed that the Church dogma of strict obedience to a harsh, judging God was wrong and that a Christian should be able to love God and obey him with a happy eagerness instead of ritual obedience. It was a passage in Paul's Epistle to the Romans that first inspired Luther in 1515: "For I am not ashamed of the gospel; it is the power of God for salvation to every one who has faith to the Jew first and also to the Greek. For in it the righteousness of God is revealed through faith for faith; as it is written, 'He who through faith is righteous shall live.'"

Luther wanted to bring the concept of individual

faith back into Christianity and to stress faith alone, without works, as the quality in man most prized by God. He also wanted to bring about a rebirth of the Bible as the authority in religion, as opposed to the Church or its tradition. He believed that man could know his sins were forgiven by God without having to seek out a priest as an intermediary, and he wanted the laity to be given a more important place in both the work and the worship of the Church.

Other reform movements, such as those of the Anglican church and John Calvin, also grew up at the same time, and although they differed from Luther's movement in the degree of their reforms, they emphasized the same general things as Luther. None wanted to cause a schism in the Church, but that is exactly what happened. Established Christianity, as it had been known in the West since the fourth century, ended after the Reformation, although not all at once.

Even though the Protestant Reformation had absorbed some of the dissatisfaction within Roman Catholicism, dissatisfaction still existed, and some countries sought to establish national Catholic churches independent from Rome. The Catholic church had become corrupt and stagnant, run in reality by greedy bishops who sought only their own gain. After the breakaway of the Protestants, dissatisfied Catholics were able to bring about reforms within the Church.

Modern Christianity

The end of the Reformation movement and the rise of Protestantism in Europe marked the beginning of the modern era of Christianity. It was an era that also saw the greatest expansion in the history of the Christian Church. This expansion was due to the exploration of the newly discovered lands, for the explorers of the sixteenth to the eighteenth century either took Christianity with them or were closely followed by Christian missionaries. By these means, the Americas were Christianized, and small Christian communities were established in Asia, Africa, and Australia.

Despite this great expansion, Christianity at the same time lost much of its prestige and authority in areas where it had long been established. During the seventeenth and eighteenth centuries the flowering of science caused scholars and scientists to look for a scientific reason for everything. As the discoveries of science continued, they came into conflict with many Christian beliefs such as the biblical account of the origin of the world and even the existence of God. But gradually the emphasis upon science and rationalism brought about toleration and religious freedom in most Western countries. It also caused those who feared the weakening of religious feeling to find ways to make Christianity more exciting and relevant. Attacks upon traditional Christian ideas helped to produce new editions of the chief documents of the Christian faith, the Bible and the writings of the reformers, and to arouse a renewed interest in the history of the Church.

The nineteenth century has been called the greatest century in the history of Christian missionary activity, both Roman Catholic and Protestant. By the very force of their attacks upon Christianity, the critics of the Church helped to bring about new attempts to reinterpret the Church in the light of the new philosophy and science. In the twentieth century, the greatest challenge to Christianity has been Communism, which held sway in Russia after the civil war called the Russian Revolution overthrew the monarchy and created the Union of Soviet Socialist Republics (Soviet Union). Under the leadership of Vladimir I. Lenin, a new system of government was introduced in which all means of production were held in common and there were no social classes. The state was all-powerful in Communism. The official Communist line on religion was atheism, or the absence of belief in a power higher than the state. Under Lenin, the Russian Orthodox Church, along with Russian royalty, was severely persecuted. Churches and church schools were closed, and all religious practices were frowned upon. In 1927, the head of the Orthodox Church in Moscow publicly expressed his loyalty to the Soviet government and refrained from criticizing the government in any way. For the next 15 years, the Church played no active role in Soviet life.

During World War II, the Soviet leader Josef Stalin revived the church, as well as other historic institutions, as a way to encourage patriotism. Churches and church schools began to function again. The Soviet Union, allied with the United States, was victorious in the war and later established its control over its Eastern European neighbors, including Poland, Hungary, Romania, and Czechoslovakia.

Roman Catholicism was very strong in these countries, and the Soviet Communists determined that the churches should not be rallying centers for resistance to the new Communist regimes they set up. By 1950, the Communist government of Poland had confiscated all lands belonging to the Catholic Church. Three years later, it demanded that all Church appointees swear an oath of allegiance to the Poland People's Republic. Similar assaults against the Roman Catholic Church occurred in the other countries in the Soviet Bloc.

Nevertheless, Catholicism did not die out under Communism; it simply went underground. Although new cities were built without churches, people continued to be "believers." The various Communist governments allowed religious celebrations, but they discouraged young people from religious practices. Since everything from college to jobs depended on membership in the Communist Party and official atheism, few young people attended church. The churches were attended primarily by old women.

By the early 1970s, there was evidence of a revival of interest in religion in the Soviet Bloc. There were more baptisms and church weddings and more young people attending church. The election in 1978 of Pope John Paul II, formerly Cardinal Karol Wojtyla, the first Polish pope, gave a major boost to the faithful living under Communist regimes, whether they were Roman Catholic or Russian Orthodox or other. When in 1980, workers at the Gdansk shipyard in Poland went on strike, they put up photographs of Pope John Paul II, showing that they felt strong in making their demands at home because one of their own was the head of the church in Rome. There was also strong religious influence in the freedom movements in Eastern Europe (East Germany, Poland, Czechoslovakia) in the late 1980s and early 1990s.

In the Soviet Union itself, liberalization under President Mikhail Gorbachev extended to religion, where church-going and religious celebrations were no longer frowned upon. In 1990, Soviet television began to air Bible cartoons supplied by the United States-based

Christian Broadcasting Network, right before the evening news.

The twentieth century has been a period of extreme activism by Christian churches. Beginning in the 1950s, black Baptist ministers in the United States led the nonviolent civil rights struggle. The Reverend Martin Luther King, Jr., the most celebrated leader of that struggle, followed the principles of nonviolent protest promulgated by Mohandas K. Gandhi in the Indian struggle for independence from Britain in the 1930s and 40s. His interest in Eastern religions foreshadowed that of Western young people in the 1960s.

As more Western young people became interested in Eastern religions like Hinduism and Buddhism, various Christian denominations attempted to reach those same young people by becoming more responsive to changing times and modern needs.

In 1962, Pope John Paul XXIII convened a Vatican Council to address the reality of a changing world. Vatican II (Vatican I had been held in 1869 to deal with the effects of the Industrial Revolution) addressed the effects of technological and scientific changes. The sixteen decrees handed down by the Council provided for masses to be said in the national languages of parishioners instead of in Latin, gave more power to bishops, committed the Church to work with other Christian faiths, and expressed the Church's position on peace and war, world poverty, industrialism, and social and economic justice.

In the United States, many priests and nuns took these decrees to mean that they should take an active role in the social movements of the 1960s, including the Civil Rights and Anti-War (or Peace) movements, which they did. A decade later, priests in Latin America as well as the United States were taking an active role in Central and Latin American freedom movements, as well as in the problem of illegal immigration. Called Liberation Theology, this movement among Catholic priests and nuns has had a strong effect on the politics of heavily-Catholic countries in the southern part of the Western Hemisphere.

Among Protestants in the United States the 1970s saw the growth of various Fundamentalist denominations and increased political activism. Fundamentalism, which arose in the United States in the nineteenth century, stresses belief in the Bible as a factual historical record and incontrovertible prophecy. The Reverend Jerry Falwell, a Baptist minister, founded a movement called the Moral Majority and sought to influence American politics by endorsing political candidates whose right-wing views against abortion and Communism and for a return to traditional moral values and patriotism had a major influence on American political life well into the 1980s. Much of that influence stemmed from the astute use of television by both Fundamentalist and Evangelical ministers. Variously referred to as the "Electronic Church" and "Televangelism," the use of television to broadcast church doctrine and raise money proved an effective use of new technology by religion. By the 1990s, scandals and charges of corruption leveled at various Fundamentalist ministers had greatly compromised their political influence and that of their movements.

The twentieth century has also seen renewed efforts to reunite the divisions in Christianity. The ecumenical (worldwide) movement has especially sought this reunion. The ecumenical movement began with Protestantism and Anglicanism, eventually included some of the Eastern Orthodox churches, and was joined to some degree by the Roman Catholic church under Pope John Paul XXIII. At Vatican II, for the first time, observers from Protestant and Eastern Orthodox churches were invited to attend and were consulted during debates. Among the decrees handed down by Vatican II were condemnations of anti-Semitism and attempts to rectify the ancient anti-Jewish record of the Church.

Pope John Paul II has expressed a deep interest in the ecumenical movement. The Catholic Church works much more closely with the World Council of Churches than it did before, although it is not a full member. John Paul II has even made speeches concerning the respect due to Islam and the need to develop spiritual bonds between Catholics and Muslims. The relationship between the Catholic Church and Judaism is problematic. The Vatican has no diplomatic relations with Israel and is often supportive of Palestinians.

If there is little chance that the various divisions of Christianity will reunite in the foreseeable future, there does exist in the Christian world a strong sense that there are many possible paths to God, that the other Christian sects as well as the other great religions are somehow related to God and may have their own, equally valid, role in God's great design.

The Main Denominations within Christianity

Roman Catholicism

Roman Catholics probably outnumber all other Christians combined. The organization of the Roman

Catholic church and its claim to authority in the Christian world rest upon the bestowal of Church authority by Jesus Christ upon Peter and his successors.

The papacy is the only institution that has existed continuously from the early Roman Empire, and it has nearly always been located in Rome. Peter did go to Rome, although he was not there very long, and he did not go there until near the end of his career. He died in Rome during the persecution under Nero. But that was enough to fix the center of the Christian Church in what was then the capital of the Roman Empire.

Because it believes itself to be the true church of Jesus Christ on earth, the Roman Catholic church cannot view other Christian traditions as equal to itself. But that does not mean that anyone outside the church cannot be saved, nor does it mean that the church does not see other Christian bodies as containing "vestiges of the Church." Catholicism is distinguished from the other forms of Christianity chiefly by three doctrines which had been discussed for centuries but were only officially decided in the nineteenth and twentieth centuries: the infallibility of the pope, the immaculate conception of Mary, and the immediate bodily assumption to heaven of the Virgin Mary upon her death without her being buried first.

Eastern Orthodoxy

Eastern Orthodoxy denies the authority of the pope to speak and act for the entire church by himself without a church council. Because of this belief, Eastern Orthodoxy has identified itself very closely with national cultures and regimes—much more so than has Roman Catholicism. But the main difference between the two churches is their attitude about the procession of the Holy Spirit from Father to Son. Roman Catholicism sees Father, Son, and Holy Spirit as three equal parts in the divine essence. The Eastern Orthodox church does not believe they are equal. Other differences are that Eastern Orthodoxy permits the clergy to marry before they are ordained as priests and that it gives the laity Communion by dipping the bread (body) in the wine (blood). In Roman Catholicism the bread and the wine are given separately.

Protestantism

The Reformation that began with Martin Luther marks the origin of Protestantism. Today there is such diversity within Protestantism that some forms have more in common with non-Protestant Christianity than they have with each other. It is difficult to accurately categorize Protestant churches and impossible to mention them all. It can be said, however, that Protestantism is basically non-Roman Western Christianity, and it can be divided into four major forms: Lutheran, Anglican, Reformed, and free (or independent) church.

Lutheranism is based on Martin Luther's teachings and its groups form the second largest Protestant membership. For the most part, Lutheran liturgy has remained traditional. The various Lutheran churches have also remained fairly isolated from other Protestant bodies.

Anglicanism is represented by the established

Church of England and churches of similar faith and order throughout the world in communion with it. The Protestant Episcopal church first came to the United States as the Church of England and then became independent. It now represents the Anglican communion in the United States. Although Anglican churches are non-Roman and allow their clergy to marry, they are unlike most other Protestant churches in that they have an episcopal system of government. Each church or parish is served by a priest who is supervised by a bishop. A bishop supervises a group of churches called a diocese. A bishop, in turn answers to a council of bishops.

The Methodist church was established by followers of John Wesley, an eighteenth-century Anglican who sought to bring about reforms within the Church of England. Wesley's movement spread to the United States in the eighteenth century and eventually became a separate church organized in an episcopal manner similar to the Anglican. The Methodist church is the largest Protestant denomination under a single government. In spite of its name, the United States-based African Methodist Episcopal Zion Church, organized in 1821 by free blacks, is Methodist in doctrine.

Presbyterian and other Reformed churches are based on the teachings of John Calvin and his followers, who were active during the Reformation, particularly in England and Switzerland. These churches are distinguished from both Lutheranism and Anglicanism by the thoroughness of their separation from Roman Catholic liturgy and doctrine. They tend to stress the sole authority of the Bible and have looked with greater suspicion than have the Lutherans and Anglicans upon the symbolic and sacramental traditions that originated before the Reformation.

Free, or independent, churches are those like the Baptist and Churches of Christ that exercise congregational government. Each congregation within these groups is autonomous, though most of them belong to a body (such as the American Baptist Convention) through which they cooperate in matters such as missions. Just as the Reformed churches go beyond Anglicanism and Lutheranism in their independence from Catholic traditions and practices, so the free churches have gone beyond the Reformed churches in rejecting remnants of Catholic traditions and practices.

The main belief of the Churches of Christ is that the Bible alone should form the basis for faith and conduct, each individual interpreting the Bible for himself and accepting no man-made creed. Each church is self-governing and responsible to no central authority. Since 1959, the Evangelical Church in the United States has been part of the Churches of Christ. In Germany and England, the Evangelical Church is part of the Reformed Church.

The Adventists are another form of free church. *Advent* means "coming," and the Adventists' distinctive doctrine centers in their belief in the Second Coming of Christ in visible form at an indefinite time. One group, the Seventh-Day Adventists, observes Saturday as the Sabbath and believes in bodily resurrection at the Second Coming of Christ. The righteous will then be rewarded with eternal life in heaven and the earth made new; the wicked will be destroyed by fire.

Other churches and movements within Christianity

include the Society of Friends (Quakers), the Universalist churches, and Christian Science.

Christian Religious Practices

Most important among Christian religious practices are the sacraments, rites or ceremonies regarded as instruments or symbols of spiritual benefit from Christ to the worshiper. The Catholic church recognizes seven sacraments—baptism, confirmation, penance, the Eucharist, matrimony, holy orders, and extreme unction. Most Protestant churches recognize only baptism and the Eucharist because these alone can be proved from Scripture to have been instituted by Christ himself.

Baptism is the rite of initiation of the Christian Church. It is almost universally recognized by all Christians, but disagreement exists over whether it should create faith or follow faith. Catholicism believes it should create faith and should therefore be performed on infants. Other groups, for example the Baptists, believe baptism should follow faith and thus be performed on teen-agers and adults.

Confirmation is the rite of admitting a baptized person into the full privileges, full membership, in the church.

Penance is the practice of repenting sin, either individually or, as in the Roman Catholic church, through confession to a priest; the performance of prayers or other payments for sin; and the receiving of forgiveness and absolution.

The Eucharist is the central rite of Christian worship. It is also called the Lord's Supper, Holy Communion, the Mass, the Divine Liturgy, and the Blessed Sacrament. It consists of repeating Christ's actions at the Last Supper, when he broke bread and passed it around as his body and passed around a cup of wine as his blood.

Extreme unction is the last sacrament, in which a dying Catholic is anointed with water blessed by a priest. Any devout Catholic can administer extreme unction.

Most forms of Christianity believe in the devil. He is the chief evil power according to the Christian faith—the adversary and tempter of man. The primary effect of man's redemption by Christ was destruction of the power of the devil, but God permits him to continue to tempt man through man's nature, his body. The souls of those men who permit themselves to be tempted, or who sin against charity and die unrepentant, go to hell, which is described as full of fire and unending. The souls of believers go to heaven, which is eternal life. Most forms of Christianity believe in both heaven and hell, but more liberal forms of Protestantism, feeling that a fiery, eternal hell is not consistent with the image of God as merciful, do not stress hell in their doctrine. Nor do they stress purgatory as does the Catholic church. Purgatory is a place or state where the souls of those who die close to God, but who have committed some sins, are detained. There the souls are cleansed and made ready for eternal union with God in heaven. There is suffering in purgatory, but there is also the possibility of the ultimate vision of God.

Although different forms of Christianity celebrate different festivals and observe different holy days, all forms observe six annual festivals—Christmas, Epiphany, Good Friday, Easter, Ascension, and Pentecost or

Whitsunday. Pentecost, Good Friday, Easter, and Ascension are related to similar festivals in Judaism and are celebrated on the same days as the Jewish festivals. Therefore, they are movable festivals, whose dates change from year to year, because the Jewish calendar differs from the Christian. Christmas and Epiphany are purely Christian festivals and occur on the same day each year.

Christmas, on December 25, marks the birth of Christ. Epiphany is celebrated on January 6 and marks both the journey of the three gentile kings to worship Jesus in Bethlehem, and his baptism. Good Friday, the Friday before Easter, commemorates Jesus' passion (suffering) on the cross. Easter marks his resurrection from the tomb. Forty days after Easter, the ascension of Christ to heaven is commemorated. Finally, Pentecost marks the descent of the Holy Spirit upon the apostles, which began the work of the Church.

Together, the various forms of Christianity make up the most widespread faith on earth—one-third of the world is Christian—and it is practiced by the widest variety of races. Almost no nation has been unaffected by Christian missions, although in some countries Christians are only a small fraction of the population. Christians can be found in nearly every Eastern country, but Christianity, from its beginnings, has remained a predominantly Western religion.

V

Islam

ISLAM DEVELOPED FROM BOTH JUDAISM AND CHRIS-
tianity and, like these religions, Islam believes that
there is one God. But while Judaism looks forward to a
son of David as the final messenger of God and Christianity sees Jesus Christ as the final messenger and
looks forward to his return, Islam sees Muhammad as
the final messenger, the last of the apostles. Islam also
considers its holy book, the Koran, as the final revelation of God's will, coming after and more perfect than
the Jewish Old Testament and the Christian New Testament.

Islam owes its existence to one remarkable man,
Muhammad, and his unique personal experience of
God. It sets man face to face with God with nothing
between them—no other gods, no priests, no ceremonies. Muhammad said, "My prayers and my wor-

ship and my life and my death are unto God, Lord of
the World. He hath no associates, and I am the first of
the Muslims."

The Life of Muhammad

The story of Muhammad's life, like that of the lives of
other great religious figures, is a combination of fact
and mythology. He was born probably between A.D. 560
and 569 to an Arab family of very high rank. His tribe,
the Banu Kinana, had been chosen by Allah (God) as
the best tribe, whose sons would be leaders of the
Arabs. Muhammad's birth and future greatness were
revealed to his grandfather, Abd al Muttalib, in a
dream. In the dream he saw a tree growing out of his
own back. Its top reached to the sky and its branches
stretched out toward east and west. A bright light radi-
ated from it, and both Persians and Arabs worshiped it.
A soothsayer who heard the dream told Abd al Mutalib
that one of his descendants would become a world
ruler and a prophet of humanity.

The true identity of Muhammad was also revealed to
his mother, Amina. When she was pregnant with
Muhammad, she sometimes heard a strange voice.
Once the voice told her that the son she was about to
bear would be a ruler and a prophet of his people.
Another time the voice commanded her to name him
Ahmad. *Ahmad* has the same meaning as *Muhammad,*
"the illustrious."

In the hour of Muhammad's birth a brilliant light
shone over the whole world and Amina was able to see
for hundreds of miles. As soon as the boy was born he

fell to the ground, scooped up a handful of earth, and looked upward toward heaven. On the night of his birth the Star of Ahmad rose in the sky, just as the Star of David shone over Bethlehem signifying the birth of Jesus.

Despite the miraculous events surrounding his birth, Muhammad's first years were quite hard. His father had died before he was born, and the widowed Amina, unable to support her child, took him to live with a family of Bedouin shepherds when he was only a few months old. But even there the miracles continued. When Muhammad was about four, he and his little foster brothers were with the sheep some distance from their tent when two angels appeared. They laid Muhammad upon the ground, opened his body, took a black drop from his heart, and washed his inner parts with melted snow from a golden vessel. Next they weighed him against ten, one hundred, and then one thousand people from his nation, but each time he tipped the scale. Finally, one angel told the other that it was useless to continue, for Muhammad would out-weigh his whole nation.

Muhammad's mother died when he was six, and his grandfather took him from the Bedouin family in order to bring him up in his house. When his grandfather died two years later, Muhammad went to live with his uncle. The young boy was loved deeply by his uncle, and because he could not bear to be separated from his nephew, the older man took the boy with him when he went to Syria with a trade caravan. The caravan had often passed by the cell of a monk named Buhaira, but this time the men of the caravan were astonished to receive an invitation to feast with Buhaira. The monk asked especially for Muhammad, for he had seen how a cloud had shaded Muhammad as he was riding in the caravan and how a tree had lowered its branches over him to shade him when the caravan had stopped at a resting place. After the monk had examined Muhammad he understood the meaning of the cloud and the tree.

When Muhammad was twenty-five, his uncle suggested that he offer his services to Khadijah, the widow of a merchant, who was sending a caravan to Syria. Muhammad did so, and again, while on the way to Syria, he was recognized as a prophet by a monk named Nestur. In Syria, with Muhammad there, the caravan's business was very successful, and Khadijah, impressed by Muhammad, and having noticed how he was shaded by two angels as he rode on his donkey, offered him her hand in marriage. She was forty years old.

By the time Muhammad was forty, he was a greatly respected man in the community and was called Al-Amin, "the reliable." He was probably a merchant, but he was not like the average merchant for he spent a great deal of time listening to the Jewish and Christian merchants and travelers who passed through the community. They told stories about the founders and great men of their religions and often argued about the merits of their various beliefs. Muhammad was intensely interested in what he heard and spent much time thinking about these religions in comparison with his.

At that time Muhammad's countrymen worshiped a number of gods who were identified by their different dwelling places—forests, trees, springs, etc. Stones were often used to symbolize and to serve as objects of worship of the different gods. The most important stone was the black stone in the Kaaba, the highest sanctuary of central Arabia, in the city of Mecca. For centuries the rectangular stone structure and the smooth black stone built into its eastern corner had been the object of pilgrimages by Arabs from many parts of the country.

As in other lands, sacrifices were the method used to establish contact with the gods, and annual sacrifices were performed to the various gods, the most important taking place at the Kaaba. Also, during certain months Arabs from neighboring areas gathered to walk around the Kaaba, beginning and ending at the sacred stone which they kissed or bowed to.

Allat, the mother of the gods, received the most worship, and in fact the other important divinities were feminine also. But there was general agreement that high over them stood a supreme god, creator and ruler of the world, who was called Allah. The Arabs called upon Allah when they were in extreme danger and made their most sacred vows in his name, but although Allah was placed in the highest position, and although Arabic-speaking Jews and Christians used the name Allah to designate their one God, the Arabs continued to worship other gods besides Allah.

Because of the influence of the Jews and Christians, Muhammad began to feel that perhaps his religion was wrong. He began to have strange dreams and bright visions. He came to love solitude and often left his home to go to the mountains and be alone with his thoughts. Once a year he spent a month in a cave on Mt. Hira performing various rites of worship.

Muhammad was in the cave on Mt. Hira when he was called to be a prophet by the angel Gabriel. He is said to have recounted the experience in this way.

He came to me . . . while I was asleep, with a coverlet of brocade whereon was some writing, and said, "Read!" I said, "What shall I read?" He pressed me with it so tightly that I thought it was death; then he let me go and said, "Read!" I said, "What shall I read?" He pressed me with it again so that I thought it was death; then he let me go and said "Read!" . . . I said, "What then shall I read?"—and this I said only to deliver myself from him, lest he should do the same to me again. He said:

"Read in the name of thy Lord who created,
Who created man of blood coagulated,
Read! Thy Lord is the most beneficent,
Who taught by the pen,
Taught that which they knew not unto men."

So I read it, and he departed from me. And I awoke from my sleep, and it was as though these words were written on my heart. . . .

When I was midway on the mountain, I heard a voice from heaven saying, "O Muhammad! thou art the apostle of God and I am Gabriel." I raised my head towards heaven to see, and lo, Gabriel in the form of a man with feet astride the horizon, saying, "O Muhammad! thou art the apostle of God and I am Gabriel." I stood gazing at him,

moving neither forward nor backward; then I began to turn my face away from him, but towards
whatever region of the sky I looked, I saw him as
before.

Muhammad was thereafter firmly convinced that
there was only one true God, Allah, and that all those
who worshiped pagan gods and lived careless lives
were in danger of harsh judgment on the last day. He
began to preach to the citizens of Mecca, warning them
that their careless living would leave them completely
unprepared for the day of judgment. Although he spoke
of the last day as if it were going to occur very soon, his
only certainty was that it would come, and he preached
that man should live, think, and act just as if the day
were visible to the eye.

Muhammad described the day very vividly. As he
envisioned it, a horrible natural catastrophe (such as an
earthquake or flood) would occur, either at the same
time as a trumpet sound calling man before the Judge
(God) or following the trumpet sound. At the first
sound of the trumpet, all men except a few elect would
fall stunned to the ground. At the second sound, all
would rise, and the dead would emerge from their
graves. The heavens would open, and Allah would appear, flanked by columns of angels. All men would go
before Allah to be judged, the good on the right and the
evil on the left. The prophets would come forth and
testify that they had proclaimed messages of warning,
and no men would be able to plead ignorance of these
warnings.

After the judgment had been passed, angels would

come and carry the good men away to paradise and a blissful existence. There would be gardens dotted with fruit trees and streams, cushions and couches to recline on, and the companionship of beautiful women.

As for the sinners, the angels would chain them and drag them away to hell. In hell, the angels would torture the sinners, forcing them to drink boiling water, crushing their arms and legs with iron clubs, clothing them in garments of fire. The accounts were horrible, and yet they did not come near to the frightfulness of some Christian descriptions of the tortures of hell.

Muhammad's conception of life after death differed greatly from the Christian conception, for while Christians see men's souls as going either to hell or paradise, Muhammad did not see the soul as an existence without a body which is able to think, feel, and act. For him, each man, body and soul, would be transported after death to paradise or hell.

In order to attain paradise and avoid hell, Muhammad preached, men must voluntarily surrender their lives to Allah. To designate this submission Muhammad used the term "Islam," and he who submitted he called a Muslim. By his own insistence, Muhammad was the first Muslim, and the messenger who had been sent to warn the Arabs.

For the first few years after his call, Muhammad stressed the day of judgment and the necessity of devotion only to Allah. He did not directly attack the pagan gods of the Qu'raish tribe, the subdivision of the Banu Kinana to which his family belonged. He preferred instead to show by example the true path the people should take. But he gained few converts by this method, and finally he began to attack their gods and to declare that all their ancestors who had died without submitting to Allah were lost. The leaders of the Qu'raish then turned against him, accusing him of seeking personal power and favor. In return, Muhammad criticized them for caring more about their own power and privilege than the salvation of their people. The conflict would intensify steadily in the next years.

As the years passed, Muhammad began to set down in writing the various "revelations" he received from Allah through the angel, Gabriel. As the revelations came to him he wrote them down on whatever was handy—pieces of parchment, tablets of wood and stone, pieces of bark, etc. A few years after Muhammad's death these revelations and the recollections of his companions would be compiled to form the holy book of Islam, the Koran.

The basic belief expressed by the Koran is that Allah is the one God and has been since the beginning of the world and will be until the end of the world. Next is the doctrine of apostles, which states that throughout history God has sent messengers to different peoples to preach the belief in one God and to warn them of the judgment that will befall them if they do not submit to Him. Most of these apostles or prophets were rejected and persecuted by their people who were thus subjected to terrible punishment by God for their lack of belief. Muslims are required to believe in all of them, although only a few are mentioned by name in their histories related in the Koran. Adam, Noah, the house of Abraham, Moses, and Jesus are especially stressed and ranked above the others. These histories often differ from the histories in the books of the Jews and Christians. Perhaps the strangest difference, at least to the Western mind, is Muhammad's ideas about the crucifixion of Jesus. Muhammad blamed the Jews for the tragedy but at the same time did not believe that it actually happened. He believed that another man was crucified in Jesus' place while Jesus was transported to paradise.

Muhammad is seen as the "Seal of the Prophets," God's apostle to all mankind. In the same way, the Koran is seen as the final revelation in a long line of revelations—the Torah was given to Moses, the Psalms are seen as being given to David, the gospel to Jesus. All are to be believed, but the Koran is to be accepted as the final revelation that clears up all uncertainties, and it discusses the truth or falsity of various Christian and Jewish beliefs.

The Koran also prescribes the rituals that Muslims should perform as part of their submission to Allah, specifically prayers and pilgrimages to the Kaaba. The Koran also contains a large body of religious and ethical teachings and laws. Wine, pigs' flesh, gambling, and moneylending, to mention a few things, are forbidden, as are a number of pagan Arab practices, specifically the making of images and idols. Rules governing marriage, divorce, inheritance, etc., are also set down. All of these rules and teachings made up the Law, and for Islam, as for Judaism and even Hinduism, the Law was seen as universal and unchanging, the Law of God.

As the years passed, Muhammad gathered a fairly large following, mostly poor Arabs who were attracted by his emphasis on generosity and consideration for the weak and by his equal application of the doctrines of judgment, paradise, and hell to all classes. But

Muhammad sought the favor of the wealthier and more powerful classes, believing that a few converts from those classes would have much more influence on the people as a whole than many conversions among the poorer classes. Later, when a decisive break came between himself and the Arab leaders, he would bitterly regret having neglected the poor who really needed him.

In one of the later revelations, Allah makes a serious indictment of Muhammad: "He [Muhammad] frowned and he turned his back, because the blind man came to him! But what assured thee [Allah asked of Muhammad] that he would not be cleansed by the faith, or be warned, and the warning profit him? As to him who is wealthy—to him thou wast all attention, yet is it not thy concern if he be not cleansed? But as to him who cometh to thee in earnest, and full of fears—him dost thou neglect!" The passage is proof of the great humility that often touched Muhammad. He was never afraid to say he was wrong.

As the conflict with the Qu'raish leaders intensified, Muhammad began to realize that he would be unable to convert the Qu'raish tribe, and he decided to go elsewhere, to some place where his doctrine would be better received. He began trying to establish alliances with various Arab chieftains who came to Mecca on pilgrimages, and in A.D. 620 he met a group of six men from the oasis of Medina who were willing to listen to him. There were many Jews in Medina, and the ideas of one God, the resurrection, and divine revelations were much more familiar to the people of Medina than to the people of Mecca. The six men quite readily believed

Muhammad's teachings and agreed to spread his message and prepare the way for him and his followers to migrate from Mecca.

About a year later, Muhammad began to send his followers in small groups to Medina until finally only he and his most loyal followers, Abu Bekr and Ali, remained in Mecca. They were being closely watched, for the Qu'raish leaders did not want Muhammad to reach Medina, realizing that he might become powerful there. Finally Muhammad, accompanied by Abu Bekr, secretly left Mecca. According to Muslim legend, when the Qu'raish went out in search of them, Allah protected them by building a dove's nest at the mouth of the cave where they were hiding. When they saw the nest undisturbed, the Qu'raish passed by the cave. After three days in the cave, Muhammad and Abu Bekr set off again and reached Medina safely. The flight to Medina, called the *hegira*, marked a turning point in Muhammad's career, a turning point so important that his followers adopted the year of the hegira, 622, as the first date of a new Islamic Calendar.

It was in Medina that Islam developed from simply a body of religious beliefs to an independent community with its own system of government, laws, and institutions. Upon his arrival in Medina, Muhammad's first concern was to have a mosque, or religious sanctuary, and under his direction his followers constructed a simple structure of sun-dried bricks. Next, he drew up a set of rules to govern the lives of his followers, who consisted of a group from Mecca and a group from Medina. Realizing the potential for conflict between the two groups, he emphasized their unity as a congregation separate from other men, and decreed that whoever caused trouble within the community should be turned upon by everyone, regardless of group—not even his relatives could support him. And in order to bring the community closer together, he caused each follower from Mecca to enter into a personal bond of religious brotherhood with a follower from Medina. These laws are the beginnings of a secular and religious constitution which gradually made Islam a world empire, a world religion, and a world brotherhood.

Medina had a large Jewish community, and at first Muhammad made a great effort to win these Jews over. His method was to make concessions to their religious customs. He commanded his followers to face Jerusalem when they prayed, and adopted some of the Jewish sacred days. But many of the Jews were not moved by Muhammad's efforts to win them over to Islam, noting that in general he deviated from Jewish customs and ideas. In the face of the Jews' criticism, Muhammad took back all the concessions he had made to their faith. Muslims should no longer face Jerusalem when they prayed; instead they should face Mecca. In this way, Muhammad not only made the Kaaba in Mecca fit in with the rest of his religious doctrine but also brought Islam nearer to the religions of all the Arabs, for they all made pilgrimages to Mecca and the Kaaba.

Medina was a city in which the cultivation of gardens was the chief means of livelihood. The gardens were already overcultivated, and the Muslims from Mecca found it hard to make a living. Therefore they turned to banditry, robbing the caravans that passed Medina on their way to and from Syria—a means of making a livelihood that was quite accepted in Medina at that time as long as it did not occur during certain holy months. In the second year after the hegira, Muhammad learned that a Qu'raish caravan was passing by. He knew that it was the month of Rajab, which the Arabs regarded as holy and during which no banditry was supposed to occur, and so he did not instruct his followers to attack the caravan. Instead, he sent Abdallah Ibn Jahsh out from the city with eight men and gave them a letter which they were to open in two days. He also told Abdallah that none of the men was to be forced to take part in the expedition proposed in the letter. Thereafter, Abdallah and six men attacked the caravan, killing one man, and captured it. It was the first bloodshed in the name of Islam.

Muhammad and his followers were strongly criticized for engaging in banditry during a holy month, and at first Muhammad insisted that he had in no way commanded such an illegal act. But after a time Muhammad announced that he had received another revelation in which Allah declared: "They will ask thee concerning war in the sacred month. Say: 'To war therein is bad, but to turn aside from the cause of Allah, and to have no faith in Him, and the sacred temple, and to drive out its people, is worse in the sight of Allah.' "

A few weeks after Abdallah's return, Muhammad learned that a large caravan involving 1,000 camels and most of the merchants of Mecca was returning from Syria. It was led by Abu Sufian, the most prominent man in Mecca and a member of the ruling family of Umayyads. Muhammad immediately led the 305 able-bodied men and 70 camels that were the extent of his resources out to attack the caravan. But Abu Sufian, wary because of previous attacks on Meccan caravans, did not pass near Medina and instead detoured toward the sea. Meanwhile, Meccan spies learned of Muhammad's plans, and the Qu'raish set out to meet his force with an army of 950 men, 700 camels, and 100 horses. When Muhammad learned that the Qu'raish were advancing, he called together the men of Medina and explained that he needed their help. The Medinians were under no obligation to fight outside their own city, but they declared their full support.

The two armies met on the eighteenth of Ramadan, in the year 2, in the Wadi Bedr, eleven miles from Medina. According to Islamic tradition, a cloud descended upon the believers and made their number seem twice as large as it was. Some said that angels dressed as warriors fought on the side of the believers; others said the angels wore green, red, and yellow turbans of light. Still others insisted that the angels fought invisibly, and that great wounds were inflicted upon the Meccan soldiers without any visible weapons. Finally, Muhammad took a handful of sand, uttered an incantation, and threw it at the enemy. The enemy soldiers fled in terror, and by noon the battle had been won.

The victory had a great effect not only upon the Meccan enemy and the people of Medina but also upon Muhammad himself, for to him it was absolute proof that Allah was on his side, and it made him decide that the rest of the Arab world must be forced to obey Allah's words and commandments. This decision began an era in which the sword was the chief missionary instrument of Islam.

In the following years, Muhammad's power in Medina increased, and finally his following was great enough so that he felt safe in planning a pilgrimage to Mecca, despite the fact that the Qu'raish sought his destruction. Accordingly, in one of the sacred months of the year 6 (March, A.D. 628), Muhammad and one thousand of his followers set out for Mecca. Because they were making a pilgrimage and thus were in a holy state, they were armed only with swords. Nevertheless, the Qu'raish considered not allowing Muhammad to enter the city, and when Muhammad heard this, he wanted to attack Mecca. But Abu Bekr reminded him that the time was one of the pilgrimage months, and when Muhammad's own camel fell to its knees and lay down, Muhammad decided that it was Allah's wish that he not attack. Instead, an agreement was made with the Meccans that the Muslims would not enter Mecca that year, but the following year the Meccans would leave the city for three days so the Muslims could carry out their pilgrimage. Muhammad's followers thought that he had made too many concessions, but Muhammad knew that an attack on the Qu'raish at that point would alienate many of those who were indecisive about joining him. And indeed, after the pact, many Arab tribes declared that they were his allies.

With greater numbers of allies, Muhammad felt able to plan a huge expedition against the Qu'raish, but this time he told no one of his plans. Even his most trusted followers did not know where Muhammad was leading them when they set out on the tenth of Ramadan in the year 8 (January, A.D. 630) with a force of ten thousand, although soon it became clear that they were on their way to Mecca. Abu Sufian, the Meccan who had led the Qu'raish forces against Muhammad, went out to meet Muhammad to negotiate a peace. Almost without knowing it, he suddenly found himself confessing his faith in Muhammad's god, Allah. After some persua-

sion, he was also able to state that he believed Muhammad was Allah's prophet. He returned to Mecca and
advised his countrymen to stay in their houses and
attempt no resistance against the Muslims.

Thus, Muhammad entered Mecca against very little
opposition. Almost immediately, he went to the Kaaba
where he touched the black stone with his staff and
cried *"Allahuakbar!"* ("God is great!"). As the cry was
taken up by his followers in a mighty chorus, Muhammad obtained the key to the sanctuary, entered, and
destroyed the idols inside. Then he spoke to the as-
sembled Muslims, telling them that the day of
paganism was past and that all blood guilt, debts, and
other obligations of the pagan period existed no more.
Then he reemphasized the sanctity of the Kaaba, saying, "No man before me was permitted to injure this
sacred place, and no man after me shall do it. I myself
have only been permitted to do it during a part of one
day."

Now Muhammad also controlled Mecca, but he was
very merciful to those who opposed him, and as a
result there were many conversions to Islam. A large
number of Arab tribes sent representatives to him and
accepted Islam, while other tribes were forced to do so
under Muslim pressure. Now essentially all of western
Arabia was under the rule of Islam.

The following year, Muhammad made a sacred pilgrimage to Mecca, fulfilling for the first and only time
the ritual which he himself had ordered for every Muslim. He spoke to his followers, declaring that a cycle
was now completed and that they had again arrived at a
point corresponding to Allah's creation of heaven and
earth. The new era would be one of good fortune and

happiness for all humanity. All Muslims were commanded to treat all other Muslims as brothers and not to injure the life or property of a brother. Further, all Muslims should fight all unbelievers until they confessed: "There is no God but Allah."

Several months after he returned from what was later to be called his farewell pilgrimage, Muhammad fell ill with a dangerous fever. According to tradition, he was commanded to go to one of the cemeteries of Medina to pray for the departed. After he had done so, he is supposed to have spoken to his liberated slave, Abu Muwaihaba, saying, "O Abu Muwaihaba! Allah offered me the key of the world and prophesied long life and Paradise thereafter, and allowed me to choose whether I desired this or to meet my Lord at once. I have chosen the latter."

Then Muhammad's illness began and lasted until the thirteenth of the month of Rabia, when he died, with the words "No, the friend, the highest in Paradise" on his lips.

Before his death, Muhammad had made no arrangements for the continued administration of the affairs of the Islamic state except that he had appointed Abu Bekr to lead the prayers. There was some confusion in Medina at first, until it was decided that Abu Bekr should be Muhammad's caliph (successor). A statement that Abu Bekr made at Muhammad's funeral reveals the quality of faith produced by companionship with Muhammad, and the quality of faith Muhammad wanted all Muslims to have: "O ye people, if anyone worships Muhammad, Muhammad is dead, but if anyone worships God, He is alive and dies not."

Islam after Muhammad's Death

For a time after Muhammad's death, the Muslim community did not engage in further conquests of territory. But after reorganizing under the caliphate of Abu Bekr, the Muslims began a new wave of conquests, sweeping over northern and eastern Arabia and beyond. Within six years after Muhammad's death, all of Arabia, Syria, and Iraq had sworn loyalty to Medina, and four years later so did Egypt. The expansion continued and in less than a hundred years the Islamic world extended over Morocco, Spain, and France to the west, and to Constantinople, across central Asia, and up the Indus River to the east.

Remarkably little destruction occurred during these conquests, and although the Muslims showed an intolerance toward other faiths, persecution was rare, and Islam proved quite willing to allow diversity within its own community. Contrary to the Christian view, Islam of that time was not the superstition of barbarians but a strong moral force that commanded respect.

Islam expanded little after its last major period of growth, chiefly because of political problems and internal religious divisions. In the tenth century, the two major sects of present-day Islam, Sunnism and Shiism, were formed. Ali, the son-in-law of Muhammad and the fourth caliph of Islam, had made his capital at Kufa in Iraq, but on his death the political center of Islam was shifted to Damascus, Syria. The Arabs of Kufa then opposed the Arabs of Syria, demanding the restoration of the house of Ali to the caliphate. But the first three caliphs, Abu Bekr, Omar, and Othman, had not been of the house of Ali, which meant that they had not held the office legitimately. This denunciation of the most revered companions of the Prophet was a great offense in the eyes of devout Muslims, who viewed the Shiites, or partisans of Ali, as heretics. Soon the Shiite name was being used to designate a wide variety of sects whose chief common element was the insistence that there existed a body of secret knowledge, supposedly given by Muhammad to Ali and by Ali to his heir, although various sects disagreed on who was Ali's heir.

Sunnism the larger and more orthodox of the two main sects of Islam, takes its name from the custom (sunna) of the Muslim community, which was not laid down in the Koran but which was handed down orally. The Koran speaks of the unchanging sunna of Allah, and both Sunnites and Shiites are loyal to the sunna of the Prophet. But the Shiites believe that the conduct of the Muslims after the Prophet's death, particularly in taking the caliphate away from the house of Ali, was illegal. Nevertheless, by 660 the caliphate was moved to Damascus, and a new dynasty, the house of Umayyads, took over the caliphate. Medina remained the center of Muslim religious learning, and the split between religious and political institutions weakened the Umayyad caliphate in A.D. 750.

Only one other major sect was to gain popularity in the next centuries—Islamic mysticism, or Sufism. Its name derived from its followers' ascetic practice of wearing undyed garments of wool (suf) as a mark of personal penitence. Sufism arose in response to the need of some Muslims for a religion that was more personal and less worldly than that practiced by the general community. Of all the great religions of western

Asia, Islam is the most worldly, condemning celibacy, rejecting the idea of priesthood, and fitting in with the secular world. Out of the need for a more personal and emotional religion, some groups of Muslims began to separate themselves from the worldly life and to become wandering beggars. Gradually they began to practice celibacy, denounced women, and began to worship saints. Gradually they also adopted the concepts of love and adoration and mystical reverence for the person of Muhammad.

Orthodox leaders soon tried to denounce Sufism, but it was too firmly based on the main teachings of the Koran and too popular among the people to be very severely criticized. And it had always been the practice of the Islamic community to tolerate the greatest freedom among its members as long as they accepted, at least outwardly, the minimum obligations of the faith. Sufism spread throughout Islam, giving the faith a more popular character and a new power of attraction. Eventually it combined with Shiism and remains part of Shiism today.

Muslim political power had many advances and setbacks over the centuries, but its religious and moral force remained strong. It encompassed a wider variety of races than any other religion until the expansion of Christian missionary activity in the nineteenth century. Even today Islam is the main religion in a wide range of territory which extends across North Africa and western Asia, eastward through central Asia into China, and then southward to Pakistan. Smaller groups of Muslims can be found in India, Malaya, the Philippines, Tanzania, the Balkan countries, southern Russia, and in both North and South America.

Modern Islamic Fundamentalism

In the second half of the twentieth century, Islamic fundamentalism gained new strength, primarily in reaction to political and economic changes in the Middle East. One major political change was the establishment of the State of Israel in 1948 and the resultant uprooting of Arab Palestinians in the area. Surrounding Arab nations, the majority of whose populations were Muslim, felt as if their territory had been invaded. Fighting between Israel and Palestinians, and between Israel and its neighbor states, has been a fact of life in the Middle East since Israel was established.

An equal, if not greater, source of tension in the Islamic world is modernization. Ever since vast oil reserves were discovered in many parts of the Middle East in the 1930s, those countries fortunate enough to have oil have become rich, resulting in efforts to modernize their industries, improve their communication and transportation networks, and build their trade with other nations. In so doing, they have had a great amount of contact with non-Islamic countries, and this contact has led to changes in their traditional cultures.

The role of women, for example, has changed as more and more women have become educated and joined the work force, leading them to question the age-old restrictions against women owning property or showing their faces in public. The role of the Muslim clergy also changed. They had enjoyed a great deal of control over the political life of the majority-Muslim states. Modernization and reforms represented, as the Ayatollah Ruhollah Khomeini of Iran once put it, "erosion of the clergy's dominance in matters of marriage, education, and morals, and the destruction of the constitutional checks and balances that kept the legislation in harmony with the Islamic law."

Iran, a non-Arab state, has a majority population of Shiites. Formerly Persia, its name was changed to Iran in 1935 by Riza Shah Pahlavi, who in 1921 had overthrown the Qajar dynasty that had ruled Persia since 1974. Riza Shah Pahlavi and later his son, Mohammed Riza Pahlavi, introduced many reforms, encouraged the development of industry, and allied themselves closely with the United States. Mohammed Riza Pahlavi recognized the state of Israel and introduced land reforms that deprived the Islamic clergy of much of their land holdings.

Khomeini, one of the most influential "ayatollahs," a title of respect that means "sign of God," in the country, bitterly opposed the shah. As a result, he was exiled in 1964. Over the next 15 years, unrest in Iran grew as common people, failing to benefit from the shah's reforms, and frightened of modernization, sought safety in traditional religious practices. The clergy encouraged them to revole against the shah, and in 1979 the shah went into exile.

Khomeini returned to Iran two weeks later. He set up a Council of the Islamic Republic of Iran, which named a prime minister who oversaw a new constitution giving Khomeini supreme power over public and military affairs. Khomeini severed relations with Israel, recognized the Palestinian Liberation Organization, and reinstituted rigid Islamic codes. Women were forced to wear the traditional head coverings. Alcoholic beverages, coeducation, mixed swimming, movies, and Western music were prohibited.

After the United States granted asylum to the shah in the fall of 1979, militant followers of Khomeini seized the American embassy in Teheran in November and took 90 hostages, 62 of them Americans. Not for 444 days were the hostages released.

Meanwhile, Khomeini urged his followers to undertake an Islamic revolution to return the world of Islam to traditional ways. On November 20, 700 armed religious militants, who had been influenced by Khomeini's Shiite revolution in Iran, seized the Grand Mosque in Mecca in Saudi Arabia. The Saudis, who are primarily Sunni Muslims, recaptured the mosque in a bloody battle in which 244 people were killed.

The following September, responding to unrest in Iraq, where the population is predominantly Shiite, the president of Iraq, Saddam Hussein, a Sunni, ordered his troops to invade Iran. The resulting war lasted for years before a cease-fire was declared with no clear winner. In the meantime, Khomeini had died, and the fundamentalist revolution in Iran was at an ebb. It and the war with Iraq had created havoc in the economy, and large segments of the population had tired of the chaos. By 1990, the government of Iran was taking steps to improve its relations with the West and was working with assorted Arab terrorist groups to effect the release of Western hostages held by those groups.

While by 1990 Islamic fundamentalism was no longer the threat it had been a decade earlier, it continues to be a major source of unrest in the Islamic world. With no strong religious leader like Khomeini, the fundamentalist revolution is being carried on by numerous independent groups. It makes for a volatile situation that affects not only the Islamic world but the rest of the world as well.

Muslim Religious Practices

The Muslim creed consists of five basic articles of faith: belief in one God, belief in angels, belief in the revealed books, belief in the prophets, and belief in the day of judgment. There are also five necessary duties: reciting the profession of faith, prayers, paying of the zakat tax, fasting, and pilgrimage to Mecca.

The profession of faith—"There is no God but Allah and Muhammad is his messenger"—must be recited at least once in each Muslim's lifetime. And it must be recited with total sincerity and total submission to God.

There are five set times for prayer in every day. Each involves a fixed number of bowings (called *rak'ahs*), and each bowing consists of seven movements with different recitations. At daybreak, two rak'ahs are required; at noon, four; at midafternoon, four; after sunset, three; and in the early part of the night, four. Ideally, prayers at the set times are performed congregationally in a mosque or "place of prostrations," but individuals must perform them also. The worshiper's face must be turned toward the Qibla, the correct direction, which Muhammad had decreed to be the Kaaba. In times of sickness or danger the ritual may be relaxed, but only in these times. The noon prayer on Friday is the chief congregational prayer of the week and work is customarily interrupted for it. After each prayer period,

the hands must be washed in a "lesser ablution."
Greater ablution is a complete washing of the body.

Every Muslim must pay the zakat tax. The term *zakat*
means "purification," and the payment of the tax
makes a Muslim's remaining property religiously and
legally pure or legitimate. It is payable on food (especially food animals), money, and the like after one
year's possession. The amount varies for different cate-
gories of taxable objects. Money from the zakat tax is to
be spent on the poor and the needy. Besides these legal
alms for the poor, voluntary and unofficial charity is
stressed in the Koran and the Muslim tradition.

The fast, during which all eating and drinking are
forbidden between daybreak and sunset, occurs during
the entire month of Ramadan, when, according to Muslim tradition, the Koran was sent down by Allah. The
Koran also states that it was sent down on the "Night of
Determination," so the Muslims observe this night on
the twenty-sixth of Ramadan. If a Muslim is sick or on a
journey, he can observe the fast period during another
equal number of days. All those who can afford it must
feed one poor man during the period.

The fifth duty is the pilgrimage *(hajj)*, and it is obli-
gatory for every Muslim with the ability and means.
Traditionally, it is performed during Dhu'l-Hijja, the
twelfth month. It consists of circling the Kaaba, assem-
bling on the ninth day of the month at the hill of Arafat,
and offering sacrifices of sheep and camels at Mina on
the way back to Mecca. All of these practices are prescribed in the Koran. Other traditional practices include kissing the black stone set in the eastern corner of
the Kaaba and stoning the pillars representing the devil

in the victory of Mina. Although these other usages are not actually mentioned in the Koran, they were observed by Muhammad in his pilgrimage and so were incorporated into the Muslim rite.

Before the pilgrimage, a Muslim must be in a state of ritual purification. He must shave his head and trade his own clothes for two plain unsewn sheets so that his head and face will be uncovered when he enters the holy territory of Mecca. After that, until his pilgrimage is over, he cannot hunt, cut his hair or nails, use perfume, cover his head, or have sexual relations. At other times of the year, it is considered meritorious to perform shorter, less ritualized pilgrimages to Mecca, which are not, however, a substitute for the hajj.

Modern Islam is very different from the simple and rigid monotheism preached by Muhammad to a small Arab community. Altogether, its community encompasses some one-seventh of the world's population, and it comprises many theological and legal schools and a great diversity of religious practices. As if it had not enough outside influences, in the last two centuries many Western ideals have pervaded its literature, education, military organization, commerce, agriculture, government, and politics. But many Muslims, while adopting what they see as good in Western culture, do not agree that Westernism is a civilizing force in the Islamic world. Instead, they emphasize Islam's role as a civilizing force in history, claiming particularly that the revival of learning and the Renaissance in Europe were due to the stimulus of Islamic culture and the borrowing of its intellectual and technical skills by European scholars and craftsmen. Whether or not Islam stimulated the revival of learning in Europe, and in spite of the fanaticism of some fundamentalist groups active today, in the long term Islam's tolerance of diversity, particularly racial diversity, sets it high among the civilizing forces in the history of mankind.

Conclusion

ALTHOUGH EACH OF THE FIVE MAJOR RELIGIONS IS DIF-
ferent from the others, all five share certain basic traits.
Each offers man a way of life which, if it is followed,
will lead to a blissful destination. Each has changed
greatly since its beginnings because of both the changing needs of its worshipers and the needs of those new
people it wished to attract.

At various points in history, each of the five religions
has been threatened because of conquest by other people, the increased influence of other religions, or by
developments in science, technology, and communications.

Of these threats, developments in scientific knowledge and communications have proved the most dangerous, especially in the West, where religions depend
so much on the existence of a personal God who actively intervenes in the affairs of man. Over the centuries, many of the questions asked by primitive man

133

about the nature of the universe, for the answers to which he turned to religion, have been answered by science.

The seventeenth century saw Johannes Kepler's studies of the motions of planets; Galileo Galilei's proof that the sun, not the earth, is the center of the universe; and Sir Isaac Newton's explanation that a single mathematical law could account for the phenomena of the heavens, the tides, and the motions of objects on the earth. These discoveries combined to give Western man an entirely different view of the world and its workings. Before these discoveries, it was universally thought that God directed the workings of the world. Now Western man realized that the world could continue with or without God. And if God was not necessary to the natural laws of the world, he was also not necessary to the moral laws—what was right and wrong.

Because of these scientific discoveries, in the eighteenth century many Westerners did not believe in a personal God who controlled the events of the world or of human life. In the nineteenth century a reaction against this lack of faith took place and there was almost a return to an age of faith. But the twentieth century has seen another time of nonbelief. Two world wars, space exploration, genetic engineering, and other events and discoveries have caused many to feel that right and wrong depend on man's purposes, not God's. Since man's purposes are different and changing, nothing in life has any real purpose. The belief is that the world is run by causes, not purposes. In the 1960s some people even suggested that God was dead. The possibility that human life has no meaning has brought great despair to the Western world.

The Eastern world has not been greatly affected by modern science, for Eastern religions have never depended upon the idea of a world directed by God or a moral world purpose. It is because Eastern religions try to satisfy the needs of people who believe that the world is not directed by God that they have attracted some Western young people to the Hare Krishna movement, meditation, yoga, and astrology.

But the tremendous upheaval in the West in the latter half of the twentieth century has also caused Westerners to turn back to the sources of their own religions, resulting in a rise in fundamentalism in Judaism, Christianity, and Islam. As we have seen, this fundamentalism has been overtly political. But the political nature of religion is nothing new. The expansion of Islam and the Crusades were political movements. The fighting in Northern Ireland between Protestants and Catholics has strong political overtones, as is the strife between Hindus and Muslims on the Indian subcontinent. Throughout history, religion and politics have been deeply intertwined.

One's religion is considered part of one's identity, and a different religion, like a different race or customs, can be seen as a threat to that identity. Ironically, at the same time as religions encourage a oneness with God or the universe, they can discourage "oneness" on earth. Religion is the creation of man and thus by nature imperfect. Yet, because of man's realization of his own imperfection, religion will always have a place in human life.

Bibliography

Andrae, Tor. *Muhammad: The Man and His Faith.* Trans. by Theophil Manzel. New York: Harper and Row, 1960.

Arvon, Henri. *Buddhism.* New York: Walker and Company, 1964.

Back to Godhead. The Magazine of the Hare Krishna Movement.

Bible, Holy. Revised Standard Version. Philadelphia: A. J. Holman. 1962.

Bouquet, A. C. *Comparative Religion.* London: Penguin Books, 1967.

Choraque, André. *A History of Judaism.* New York: Walker and Company, 1964.

Coomaraswamy, Ananda K. *Buddha and the Gospel of Buddhism.* New York: Harper and Row, 1964.

Davis, W. D. *Invitation to the New Testament.* New York: Doubleday, 1969.

Haskins, James. *Leaders of the Middle East.* Hillside, NJ: Enslow Publishers, 1985.

Krishnamurthy, V. *Essentials of Hinduism.* New Delhi: Narosa Publishing House, 1989.

Nichols, Peter. *The Pope's Divisions: The Roman Catholic Church Today.* London: Faber and Faber, 1981.

Roberts, D. S. *Islam: A Concise Introduction.* San Francisco: Harper & Row, 1981.

Seeger, Elizabeth. *Eastern Religions.* New York: Crowell, 1973.

Simpson, John. *Inside Iran.* New York: St. Martin's Press, 1988.

Smith, Hedrick. *The Russians.* New York: Ballantine Books, 1976.

Wright, Robin. *Sacred Rage: The Wrath of Islam.* New York: Simon and Schuster, 1985.

Index